The American History Series

SERIES EDITORS

John Hope Franklin, *Duke University*
Abraham S. Eisenstadt, *Brooklyn College*

Arthur S. Link

Princeton University

GENERAL EDITOR FOR HISTORY

ρ

Reginald Horsman

The University of Wisconsin—Milwaukee

The Diplomacy of the New Republic,

1776–1815

Harlan Davidson, Inc.

Arlington Heights, Illinois 60004

Library of Congress Cataloging in Publication Data

Horsman, Reginald.
    The diplomacy of the new republic, 1776–1815.

    (The American history series)
    Bibliography: p. 131
    Includes index.
    1. United States—Foreign relations—1783–1815. 2. United States—Foreign relations—Revolution, 1775–1783. I. Title.
II. Series: American history series (Harlan Davidson, Inc.)
E310.7.H77   1985   327.73   84-23691
ISBN 0-88295-829-1

Cover illustration: Courtesy, The Henry Francis du Pont Winterthur Museum. Detail from painting.

FOREWORD

Every generation writes its own history, for the reason that it sees the past in the foreshortened perspective of its own experience. This has certainly been true of the writing of American history. The practical aim of our historiography is to offer us a more certain sense of where we are going by helping us understand the road we took in getting where we are. If the substance and nature of our historical writing is changing, it is precisely because our own generation is redefining its direction, much as the generations that preceded us redefined theirs. We are seeking a newer direction, because we are facing new problems, changing our values and premises, and shaping new institutions to meet new needs. Thus, the vitality of the present inspires the vitality of our writing about our past. Today's scholars are hard at work reconsidering every major field of our history: its politics, diplomacy, economy, society, mores, values, sexuality, and status, ethnic, and race relations. No less significantly, our scholars are using newer modes of investigation to probe the ever-expanding domain of the American past.

Our aim, in this American History Series, is to offer the reader a survey of what scholars are saying about the central themes and issues of American history. To present these themes and issues, we have invited scholars who have made notable contributions to the respective fields in which they are writing. Each volume offers the reader a sufficient factual and narrative account for perceiving the larger dimensions of its particular subject. Addressing their respective themes, our authors have undertaken, moreover, to present the conclusions derived by the principal writers on these themes. Beyond that, the authors present their own conclusions about those aspects of their respective subjects that have been matters of difference and controversy. In effect, they have written not only about where the subject stands in today's historiography but also about where they stand on their subject. Each volume closes with an extensive critical essay on the writings of the major authorities on its particular theme.

The books in this series are designed for use in both basic and advanced courses in American history. Such a series has a particular utility in times such as these, when the traditional format of our American history courses is being altered to accommodate a greater diversity of texts and reading materials. The series offers a number of distinct advantages. It extends and deepens the dimensions of course work in American history. In proceeding beyond the confines of the traditional textbook, it makes clear that the study of our past is, more than the student might otherwise infer, at once complex, sophisticated, and profound. It presents American history as a subject of continuing vitality and fresh investigation. The work of experts in their respective fields, it opens up to the student the rich findings of historical inquiry. It invites the student to join, in major fields of research, the many groups of scholars who are pondering anew the central themes and problems of our past. It challenges the student to participate actively in exploring American history and to collaborate in the creative and rigorous adventure of seeking out its wider reaches.

John Hope Franklin

Abraham S. Eisenstadt

CONTENTS

Introduction

In the years from 1775 to 1815, the United States sought political independence, security, and commercial and territorial expansion. Independence was won by 1783, but both security and the prospects for expansion were threatened by the weakness of the central government under the Articles of Confederation. The government failed to secure hoped-for trade agreements with Great Britain and Spain, and in the Mississippi Valley the power of the central government was insufficient to cope with Indian resistance or with the British and Spanish presence and influence within American territory. In the 1780s, while some Americans still dreamed of widespread expansion, others feared that the republic would fall apart under the pressure of external enemies and internal weakness.

The new constitution and the establishment of a more powerful central government in 1789 did much to lessen threats to American security and made possible the shaping of policies to further the commercial and territorial expansion dreamed of since before the Revolution. Yet, in the course of the 1790s, sharp political disagreements emerged regarding how a safe, prosperous, and expanding nation could be ensured. Hamilton and the Federalists thought that American prosperity could be fostered by close commercial ties with Great Britain. Jefferson and his Democratic-Republicans feared that such ties would encourage monarchical ideas in America and corrupt the republic. They also believed that the interests of America's farmers could best be served by an expansion of markets outside the British Empire, and that the future of an agrarian republic depended upon a vigorous pursuit of westward expansion.

The political differences concerning the conduct of American foreign policy were much increased by the extensive wars that swept Europe from 1783 to 1815. These wars brought both opportunities and dangers to the United States: opportunities in that the preoccupation of the European powers gave the new and more powerful central government the chance to obtain secure boundaries, access to the Gulf of Mexico, and a huge area of territory in the Mississippi Valley; but dangers in that the expansion of commerce generated by the wars was accompanied by widespread interference with American shipping. Both England and France disputed the American claim that a neutral could trade freely in time of war. The Federalists and Democratic-Republicans argued bitterly in deciding how to respond to European interference with American trade. The Federalist determination to maintain close relations with Great Britain in spite of all provocations led to an estrangement from France in the late 1790s; and the Democratic-Republican resentment at British commercial policies was the primary cause of a second war with England in 1812.

The United States was ill-prepared for the War of 1812 and narrowly escaped disaster, but by 1815 all of the objectives that had been sought since 1775 were within America's grasp. Political independence and security had been achieved, and the United States was poised for dramatic territorial and commercial expansion. That this had proved possible stemmed partially from America's distance from Europe and from Europe's preoccupation with its own struggles, but it also arose from the skill with which the early American leaders had managed to shape a federal union out of disparate colonies. By 1815 the time of constant crisis had passed, and a century of dramatic expansion had begun.

ONE

Freedom
and Expansion

When the American colonists sought help from foreign nations in the first years of the American Revolution, they brought with them attitudes and beliefs that had evolved in over one hundred and fifty years of colonial history. They also brought with them a firm belief in their innate power. The early American leaders confronted the rest of the world with sophistication and confidence. They did not act like desperate men, willing to grasp at any straw or willing to give any concession to gain aid for their struggle against Great Britain; they acted like men who were quite confident of America's importance in the world and of the likelihood of its future greatness. Great anxiety arose in the United States in the years after the American Revolution, not because of doubts about the country's inherent potential for greatness, but rather because of the fears that it would not prove possible to create a republican government that would weld together a mighty continent.

At the heart of American confidence at the beginning of the Revolution was the remarkable material growth that had taken place in America since the first English settlers had gained a precarious foothold on the continent at the beginning of the seventeenth century. One hundred and fifty years earlier there had been struggling settlements in Virginia and at Plymouth, but by 1775 there were thirteen colonies with a population of some two and a half million people strung along the American seaboard from Maine to Georgia. In the years immediately before the Revolution, American pioneers had begun to cross the Appalachians to place settlements in what is now eastern Tennessee and in the bluegrass region of Kentucky. Some in the East saw this as the beginning of a process that would encompass the continent.

By the middle of the eighteenth century, the idea that the English settlements in America were destined to embrace most of the continent was well-engrained in American and European thinking. For many observers, America held out the hope for a progress that would be difficult to attain in the decadent Old World, and many believed that the population growth and prosperity of the eighteenth century was only just the beginning. Benjamin Franklin prophesied in 1751 that in time there would be more Englishmen in America than in England. He believed that the American population would double every twenty-five years. John Adams also thought that the population of the American colonies one day would exceed that of Great Britain, and he suggested that "the great seat of Empire" might be transferred to America in the future.

Accompanying the expectation of a constantly expanding and prospering American population was the more immediate and practical confidence produced by the abundance of agricultural products and raw materials which were sold to England in great quantities, and the development of a dynamic American merchant marine which prospered on the carrying of goods and slaves within the extensive British empire. The American leaders were supremely confident that the commerce of the American colonies was of vital importance to Great Britain and would be of vital importance to the rest of the world. In December 1776, when Congress discussed why it would be in France's interest to support a separation of the American colonies from England, it was said that Great Britain "would at once be deprived of one third of her power and Commerce." The Americans of the revolutionary generation believed that their commerce could be a weapon powerful enough to manipulate the powers of Europe.

Material success and prosperity gave confidence to America's leaders at the beginning of the Revolution, but this success and the Revolution itself were given an additional special meaning by the pervasive American sense of mission and destiny. This sense of mission had its roots deep in the seventeenth century. The settlers of New England had brought with them a militant Puritanism. From the time of their first settlements they had conceived of themselves as chosen by God for special work. They were to be an example to the world, and a means by which the world could be regenerated. This sense of mission and destiny never disappeared from American thought in the colonial years, although in the eighteenth century it entwined with a more secular belief in progress that was fed by the ideas of the European Enlightenment and by the example of America's burgeoning prosperity.

The Revolution gave this sense of destiny a whole new dimension; after declaring independence the Americans saw themselves in a struggle to liberate mankind from corrupt, tyrannical monarchies and despotisms through the expansion of republicanism. Even before the Declaration of Independence, English immigrant Thomas Paine eloquently expressed this American sense of destiny and confidence in his pamphlet *Common Sense,* a work that helped inspire the colonists to believe that the ties with England should be broken. "The cause of America," he wrote early in 1776, "is in a great measure the cause of all mankind." In this revolutionary era most Americans were able to convince themselves that what was good for America was good for the world.

THE BEGINNINGS
OF REVOLUTIONARY DIPLOMACY

The first efforts of the American revolutionaries to establish diplomatic contact with foreign nations were forced on them by the growing crisis with England in the year and half following the outbreak of the American Revolution in April 1775. In the months following the beginning of fighting in Massachusetts, many colonists hoped that English concessions or a willingness to negotiate would bring about a reconciliation, but as the British hastened to raise armies to quell the revolt it became apparent that the American colonies would need outside assistance. The most obvious necessities were arms and ammunition, but it was also clear that if the American colonists were to resist one of the most powerful countries in the world, more general support would be needed.

In seeking such support, the American colonies were obliged to overcome, at least temporarily, foreign rivalries that had grown throughout the colonial era, during which the colonists had combined with Great Britain to fight a series of wars against France, and in which there had been major conflicts with the Spanish. While necessity drove the American colonies into the arms of France, and raised hopes of an agreement with Spain, long-standing conflicts of interest with these powers were to cause friction before the Revolution ended.

As early as September 1775, the Continental Congress created a secret committee to arrange for the importation of arms and ammunition, and late in November it established a committee of secret correspondence, which had the task of investigating the possibility of more formal and extensive foreign support. This committee of secret correspondence became the committee of foreign affairs, but until the end of the 1780s the nature of the American government prevented any cohesive direction of foreign policy. As an alliance of separate states, the Continental Congress conducted its business through committees, and while the committee of secret correspondence had a continuous existence until 1781, other committees were also created to deal with particular problems. While the instructions written by these committees had to be approved by the whole Congress, these documents differed in thrust, depending upon the membership of a particular committee or on who actually wrote the draft.

American leaders in 1775–1776 never had any doubt that France offered the best hope for aid in the struggle against England. Since the last quarter of the seventeenth century, France and England had waged a series of wars that involved much of Europe as well as distant colonial areas. The last of these struggles, known in America as the French and Indian War, ended in 1763 with France's loss of Canada as well as other possessions around the world. For most of the eighteenth century the Americans feared French encirclement and competed with French Canada for the control of the trans-Appalachian fur trade, but at the beginning of the Revolution Congressional leaders realized that France's desire for revenge on England offered America's best hope for assistance. They also believed that apart from any desire for revenge, France would be seduced by the chance to break up the British-American commercial system and prosper on American trade.

In the winter of 1775–1776, Congress proceeded cautiously because it still hoped for British concessions and reconciliation, but beginning in late 1775 it made efforts to sound out the intentions of England's European rivals. At first Congress made use of a Virginian, Arthur Lee, who had been the Massachusetts agent in London, but in March 1776 Silas Deane of Connecticut was sent to Paris to make a more determined effort to obtain French aid. As the colonies still had not declared their independence, Deane travelled not as an envoy of the American colonies but in the guise of a merchant. France, of course, did not need American suggestions to understand the advantages to be gained from fanning the flames of discontent across the Atlantic, and made a decision in the spring of 1776 to provide secret assistance to the revolutionaries. Under the direction of the scintillating politican and playwright Caron de Beaumarchais, who was eager to help the Americans, a trading company was created to provide a front for the shipment of arms and ammunition across the Atlantic. Spain also used the same cover to provide secret help.

While France was moving towards the decision to provide aid, the American Congress in these early months of 1776 was debating measures which would widen the gulf between America and England. A key issue was the question of commerce. To this point the American colonies were still formally enclosed in the British commercial system, but Congress now moved toward throwing off British commercial regulations. With Great Britain showing every intention of pursuing a military solution to America's complaints, unrestricted trade with other countries appeared to be a necessity, but opening such trade presented immediate military problems. In February 1776, Roger Sherman of Connecticut suggested that if the colonies opened up their trade with other nations, then a treaty with a foreign power would be necessary to provide protection from British depredations. Going even further, George Wythe of Virginia argued that if the colonies offered trade to other countries, then, to get these countries to take America seriously, the colonists would have to declare themselves "a free people."

The impetus toward opening up trade with all nations, obtaining overt foreign help, and establishing independence was increased by the publication of Thomas Paine's *Common Sense* early in 1776. Paine suggested that it was in the interest of Europe to have America as "a *free port*," and that commerce could secure America "the peace and friendship of all Europe." Paine also argued, falsely, that it was only the English connection that dragged the colonies into conflict with France and Spain. America's interest, he argued, was "to steer clear of

European contentions.'' It was absurd, wrote Paine, for a great continent to be subject to a little island; America's connection with Europe should be merely that of trade.

In April 1776, the American colonies opened up their trade to all nations, and some states and many individuals were now pressing Congress to take the decisive step of declaring American independence from England. On June 7, 1776, Richard Henry Lee of Virginia proposed that the colonies should be independent, stating ''it is expedient forthwith to take the most effectual measures for forming foreign Alliances,'' and that ''a plan of confederation'' should be prepared and submitted to the individual colonies. Independence, alliances, and union marched together. Lee believed that the United States needed foreign alliances but that they would not be possible until the colonies had severed their relations with Great Britain. It was soon quite apparent that many members of Congress thought of foreign alliances only as a means of obtaining aid and opening up commercial opportunities, not as a mutual commitment to specific political or military actions. Felix Gilbert has argued that in assuming that this was possible Americans were merely reflecting the ambiguities of eighteenth-century usage, in which ''alliance'' could have a variety of nonpolitical meanings.

In response to Lee's resolves Congress appointed separate committees to draft a declaration of independence, to develop a plan of union, and to prepare a model treaty which would in the first instance be offered to France. Out of the first came Thomas Jefferson's Declaration of Independence, out of the second the plan for government under the Articles of Confederation, and out of the third a treaty draft that was written by John Adams. The draft was written by July, discussed and amended in Congress in August, and prepared in its final form in September. The final document revealed both the extent to which the Americans were convinced of the vital importance to European nations of American trade, and the nature of America's territorial ambitions on the North American Continent. This model treaty was a remarkable document. The American representatives were not to go cap in hand to beg the assistance of the mighty French; rather they were to offer the French the inestimable prize of trade with America if the French would agree to provide aid to the colonists and would agree to American claims to all British possessions on the North American Continent. Some historians (most notably Felix Gilbert) have argued that the model treaty of 1776 represented an idealistic effort to achieve international peace through free trade. There seem to be more reasons to accept the arguments of such historians as James Hutson who see the treaty as a more practical effort to use commerce as a political weapon within the European and trans-Atlantic balance of power. Perhaps most of all the model treaty reveals the optimism with which John Adams and his American compatriots viewed the prospects of the infant nation at the moment of its birth. The model treaty is a supremely confident document, and only when the trials of the Revolution and the difficulties of creating an effective union later became uppermost was American confidence temporarily replaced by a deep-seated fear that the great republican experiment might fail.

In the model treaty, Adams suggested that French aid and mutual trade could be obtained without any entangling commitment on the part of the Americas. In this he was in accord with Benjamin Franklin and Thomas Paine; they also both believed in these early months of the Revolution that the friendship of European powers could be secured through the bait of American commerce. Adams's basic commercial suggestion was that the American colonies and France should treat the ships and citizens of the other country as they treated their own. This might not mean completely free trade, but neither French nor American citizens would be discriminated against in each other's ports. Moreover, Adams and Congress decided that they wanted to write into the treaty a very liberal description of how neutrals could trade in time of war.

In the course of the eighteenth century, countries with large fighting navies, particularly England, had tried to restrict neutral trading in time of war. Smaller nations, or nations with less naval power, had generally tried to gain acceptance of the idea that neutrals could trade quite freely in wartime. The new

America enthusiastically sought a high degree of freedom for neutral trade. The Americans wanted the list of contraband goods, which all powers agreed could be seized, to be kept short and limited; they wanted freedom to trade between the ports of a country at war; and they urged acceptance of the doctrine that "free ships make free goods." By this last provision even the goods of a country at war could escape seizure if carried on a neutral vessel. By the provisions of the model treaty the American states wished to expand markets for their agricultural produce outside the British system, provide for an increase in their carrying trade, and ensure that such exporting and carrying could continue even in time of European war.

Along with hoping to achieve a commercial connection with France, and to receive some of the necessary military supplies for waging war against Great Britain, the Americans also wanted to be given a free hand on the North American Continent. France was to renounce any effort to take or regain territory on the mainland. To be quite sure there was no mistake, the details of the proposed French renunciation were spelled out in article IX of the model treaty. In this article it was stated that the French king would promise never to "invade, nor under any pretence attempt to possess himself of Labradore, New Britain, Nova Scotia, Acadia, Canada, Florida," nor any of the countries or towns on the continent of North America or the islands nearby. The American colonies reserved to themselves the right to all areas on the continent, or nearby islands, which were or lately were under the jurisdiction of Great Britain. It was understood that France could take the British West Indies, but if this happened then the other portions of the commercial agreement would apply to American trade to those islands.

Article IX of the model treaty revealed quite clearly that along with a dream of American commerce expanding outside the British system to all the nations of Europe, Adams envisaged an expanding nation on the North American Continent. This assumption was shared by many others besides Adams, and from the very beginning of the Revolution the Americans had tried to provide for their future security by ensuring that Canada would become part of their new nation. As early as October 1774, the colonists had asked Canada to join in the resistance to Great Britain, stating that theirs was "the only link wanting to compleat the bright and strong chain of union." The appeal was renewed in the spring of 1775, and when it produced no response, the colonies launched an invasion of Canada in September 1775, before they had declared their independence from Great Britain. The invasion almost succeeded, but the Americans failed to capture Quebec late in the year. Canada was deemed essential to American security, and it was well-understood that the incorporation of Canada into the new nation would eliminate any possible renewal of the old rivalry for the fur trade and the lands of the trans-Appalachian West.

That American ambitions went beyond the removal of an immediate British threat from Canada was shown quite clearly in the Congressional debates and diplomatic papers of the Revolutionary era. It was assumed that the elimination of European possessions in North America was only a matter of time. In the debates in Congress following Richard Henry Lee's motion for independence, foreign alliance, and union, a speaker who doubted America's ability to make alliances said that the colonies had little reason to expect an alliance because "France and Spain had reason to be jealous of that rising power which would one day certainly strip them of all their American possessions." The answer given to this was that the "rising power" of the colonies would be far more threatening to France and Spain if it continued to be in coalition with Great Britain.

In September 1776, when Congress decided to send Benjamin Franklin to Europe to join Silas Deane and Arthur Lee in an effort to sign a formal agreement with France, and to obtain more aid, the fighting was becoming critical for the United States. British forces in New York were poised to attack Washington's army, and some Americans were questioning whether the colonies could maintain their independence through the following winter. Yet, even in this time of crisis, Congress still hoped that the offer of American trade would persuade France to sign a treaty that would contain no commitments by the

United States. Congress realized that there might be difficulty in obtaining a formal agreement, but in the instructions which Franklin took with him to France, the American commissioners were given little flexibility. If France proved reluctant to sign a treaty, then the commissioners could modify the commercial agreement. Instead of each power treating the other's citizens as their own for purposes of trade, the commissioners could propose a "most-favored nation" agreement, by which each would grant the other at least the commercial concessions given to other nations. The Americans still seemed to expect that the prospect of American trade would be enough to bring a formal agreement with France.

The commissioners were also empowered to approach other European powers, but once again the new America wanted European help without European entanglement. The flexibility given to the commissioners was extremely limited. The major concession that was allowed was that if Spain appeared disinclined to support the American cause because of fear for the safety of her South American possessions, then the United States would promise not to molest them. The newly independent states were conducting themselves not as weak ex-colonies in danger of collapse but rather as a power which was ready and able to threaten all European possessions in the New World.

The dangerous situation of the American colonies in the fall of 1776 did not diminish the belief that the surrounding areas on the North American Continent would eventually be acquired. Before leaving for France, Benjamin Franklin drew up a draft of possible terms for a future peace with Great Britain. Essential for America's interest, he believed, was the acquisition of Quebec, St. John's, Nova Scotia, Bermuda, East and West Florida, and the Bahamas, "with all their adjoining and intermediate territories." "It is absolutely necessary for us to have them," he wrote, "for our own security." Franklin, who was nearing the end of a distinguished career spent mostly within the confines of the British empire, had thought in terms of expansion on the North American Continent since long before the

American Revolution. Up to 1775, he had thought of American territorial and commercial expansion as contributing to the power and dominance of a wider-reaching Great Britain, but in his last years he thought of it more in terms of security and an expanding American republicanism. As a commissioner in Europe, Franklin strove to obtain for the United States the breadth of territory he thought necessary for her future progress.

At the age of seventy, Franklin was already famous throughout Europe, and as the representative of the new America, he skillfully won the hearts of the Parisians. Affecting a plain, republican style, which served to divert attention from his guile, Franklin turned all his efforts to winning overt French aid.

By the time that Franklin joined Deane and Lee in Paris in December 1776, Congress had decided that French help was so essential that the ideal of American freedom from commitment would have to be modified. Washington had been obliged to retreat from New York across New Jersey into Pennsylvania, and in expectation of a British attack Congress left Philadelphia and reconvened in Baltimore. At the end of December the committee of secret correspondence informed the commissioners that Congress now deemed "the speedy declaration of French and European assistance so indispensably necessary to secure the independence of these States" that it was willing to authorize concessions it was hoped would bring about an agreement. Congress had decided that if the offer of a commercial agreement was not enough to get France into the war, then the commissioners could promise American aid in any French attempt to capture the British West Indies. Congress also decided that if Spain would join in the war, the United States would help it retake Pensacola from the British, provided that the citizens and inhabitants of the United States should have "the free and uninterrupted navigation of the Mississippi and use of the harbour of Pensacola." In 1763, at the Peace of Paris, Spain had been obliged to cede to Britain the Floridas, which then included not only modern Florida but also a strip of territory along the Gulf to the Mississippi. Spain was anxious to reconquer the area, but knew full well that the new United States also desired the same region because of the access that it provided to the Gulf of Mexico.

Even at the bleakest time of the Revolution, the American states kept a clear vision of the nature of the independence they were seeking. Although they had been driven into a willingness to promise commitments in an effort to gain French and Spanish assistance, they still sought agreements and an eventual victory which on one hand would expand American commercial opportunities throughout Europe and on the other would give the United States the territory westward to the Mississippi and free access to the Gulf of Mexico.

The right for the Americans to navigate the Mississippi to its mouth beyond New Orleans was becoming of vital importance as American pioneers crossed the Appalachians and penetrated the eastern half of the Mississippi Valley. Settlers were in east Tennessee by the late 1760s and on the eve of the Revolution had plunged into the bluegrass region of Kentucky. Even the terrors of combined British-Indian attacks in the Revolution could not stop the expansion of these settlements, and in the middle of the Revolution a party of settlers had established a bridgehead in central Tennessee at what is now Nashville. These trans-Appalachian settlers could not send their produce eastward over the mountains—the long journey was too difficult and too costly. The only feasible route to market was to follow the tributaries of the Mississippi to that river and down to New Orleans. In the years after the Revolution, even the farmers of western Pennsylvania were to find it more practical to send their produce many hundreds of miles downriver to New Orleans by water than to try to ship goods eastward over the mountains to Philadelphia. From the beginning of the Revolution, the members of Congress assumed that the Indian lands westward to the Mississippi were to be taken by the new United States and that the free navigation of the Mississippi was essential to the welfare and prosperity of the settlers who would develop the new lands. If Spain held New Orleans and the mouth of the river, then somehow Spain would have to be persuaded to grant navigation rights.

Late in December, when Franklin, Deane, and Lee communicated to the French Foreign Minister, Vergennes, the news that they had been empowered to negotiate for the United States, they persisted in the attitude that the United States was conferring a benefit rather than asking for help. They said that they were empowered to negotiate "a treaty of amity and commerce," and that the generous treatment American ships had received by free admission into French ports, together with other marks of respect, had "induced the Congress to make this offer first to France." In reality, the United States desperately needed French or Spanish aid, and throughout 1777 the American commissioners tried to lure those powers into an agreement. France and Spain continued to supply needed arms and ammunition, but they avoided committing themselves to a formal treaty. In general, the new United States discovered that rather than welcoming American trade with open arms, most European countries were wary of doing anything that would offend powerful Great Britain until they were sure that the American colonies would offer more than token resistance to British force.

The tenacity of Washington's army and the great difficulties that the British experienced in campaigning on the North American Continent worked against any quick British victory. British difficulty in bringing a quick end to the war became more and more apparent in 1777, and a major turning point of the Revolution was reached in October when General John Burgoyne's attempt to invade the United States from Canada resulted in the surrender of his whole army at Saratoga. This striking American victory removed the last French doubts. Fearful that the British might now win back American allegiance by large-scale concessions, and anxious to weaken Great Britain, France decided to make the Anglo-American break irreparable by allying with the Americans. Spain, however, fearful that an independent American republic would threaten its American possessions, refused to enter into an alliance.

FRENCH ALLIANCE AND INDEPENDENCE

On February 6, 1778, France and the United States signed two treaties—one a treaty of amity and commerce, the other a treaty of alliance. The latter treaty was to come into force if, as expected, Great Britain and France should go to war because of the first treaty. The United States had hoped to achieve formal French aid merely by signing the first; the second had become necessary because of French unwillingness to sign an agreement that contained no American commitments. The first treaty was a slightly modified version of the American model treaty plan of 1776. The basic commercial agreement between the two countries granted "most-favored nation" status, not the freer trade that Adams had envisaged in his model treaty, but the provisions regarding neutrals in wartime followed the suggestions of the model treaty; included were extensive guarantees of the neutral right to trade with belligerents. France was willing to accept the American definitions in this regard because France's main enemy—Great Britain—had the naval power to cripple French commerce in time of war. The Americans wanted to include provisions for neutral trade in time of war because they were anxious to send their exports and carrying trade to every corner of Europe and the world, whether in peace or war.

By the treaty of alliance the United States promised that France could keep any British West Indian islands that France conquered. The treaty also guaranteed French possessions in the New World, and it was agreed that no separate peace would be signed. In reality, however, the United States conceded little of substance in the treaty of alliance, and in return gained not only French aid and a commercial agreement but also French recognition of American rights on the North American Continent. The French agreed that the United States could keep any British possessions it conquered in the northern parts of America, including the Bermudas. France permanently renounced possession of territory on the mainland that it had owned before 1763, as well as the Bermudas, and agreed to sign no peace until American independence had been achieved.

Lawrence S. Kaplan has suggested that the United States, in signing the alliance of 1778, was obliged to abandon the nonentanglement principles it had expounded in 1776. It can be argued, however, that the United States had achieved most of its immediate aims without overly extensive commitments. The United States had secured French aid, a recognition of independence, an acknowledgment of its right to all British possessions in North America, a commercial agreement, and French recognition of the American interpretation of neutral rights in wartime. In return, the treaty acknowledged the French right to the British West India islands, if France could conquer them, guaranteed French possessions in the New World, and committed the United States to a "permanent" alliance with France. Later, those parts of the treaty that did not suit American interests were ignored. In 1782, in the face of French unwillingness to press for all the territory it desired, the United States signed a separate peace agreement with Great Britain, and in the 1790s, American policies favored the British much more than the French.

In the immediate aftermath of the signing of the French alliance, Benjamin Franklin and even John Adams were optimistic that close links with France would work to the benefit of the United States. In December 1777, Adams had been appointed to replace Silas Deane in the American commission to France. Although the appointment of Adams added great talent to the American mission, it also added great tension. New Englander Adams was a man of intelligence and honesty, but he was also aloof, vain, and inordinately suspicious of those around him. Adams instinctively disliked the easy-going, pleasure-loving Franklin.

In Adams's first months after his arrival in France, he temporarily modified his 1776 view that all entanglements with

European nations should be avoided. Buoyed by the advantages that had been gained by the French alliance, he argued in July 1778 that America could best resist English power by a permanent alliance with France. Only France, he believed at this time, could offer the necessary counterweight to British strength. Adams thought that at the heart of America's problems were the adjacent British possessions in North America, for "neighboring nations are never friends in reality." As France was also a natural enemy of Great Britain, France and the United States had a natural compatibility of interests and France was "the natural ally" of the United States. "As long as Great Britain shall have Canada, Nova Scotia, and the Floridas, or any of them, so long will Great Britain be the enemy of the United States, let her disguise it as much as she will."

The danger presented by Canada was also very evident to General Washington. In May 1778, he wrote that the accession of that area to the union was "a measure much to be wished." He perceived danger in Canada's proximity to the eastern states and in its connection with the western Indians. The threat to American security posed by the British presence in Canada was a constant theme of the early years of the American republic. Not until American population growth and the increase in American strength took away the danger from British machinations within American territory were the Americans to lose this feeling of pressing crisis.

Adams's temporary conviction that British maritime and territorial power necessitated a close agreement between the United States and France was shattered in the following years. In negotiating with French foreign minister Vergennes he soon became convinced that France, like England before her, was working to keep the United States in a position of dependency. Adams had ample reason for reaching this conclusion, for France had no interest in erecting a powerful nation on the other side of the Atlantic. France aided the revolution in order to reduce England's power; when it became apparent that the colonists would win independence, France's wish was to limit American power and to bring the United States clearly within the French sphere of influence. In the last years of the Revolution, Adams returned to his original desire of 1776; that the United States should pursue an independent course, controlled by neither the British nor the French. In advocating this course he frequently clashed with Franklin, for he perceived Franklin as too much under French influence. In reality, Franklin, like Adams, wished to provide for the security, expansion, and prosperity of the United States. He retained longer than Adams, however, the faith that this could be secured by working closely with the French.

In October 1778, when Congress decided to appoint Franklin minister to France, it also supplied him with fresh instructions. The most important section of the instructions related to a plan for the conquest of Canada. The United States wanted France to cooperate in the capture of Halifax and Quebec, and submitted a general plan suggesting how this could be accomplished and listing the advantages to both countries. The conquest of Canada, it was argued, would give the United States two new states (Quebec and Nova Scotia), establish peace on the frontiers, help its finances, and secure its commerce. France, Congress suggested, would gain a share in the Newfoundland fisheries, extend commerce, and regain a share of the fur trade. How the last was to be accomplished was left obscure. In any case it was all in vain. France had no desire to see the removal of all threats in North America to the security of the United States, for this would free the new republic from dependency upon the French. France did nothing to further the American plans for the conquest of Canada, and during the rest of the war the United States waited in vain for French help for a northern invasion.

The Floridas and the navigation of the Mississippi presented a similar problem of desire exceeding capability. Spain knew full well that the Americans had designs upon the whole Gulf region to the Mississippi River, and above all else wanted free navigation of that waterway, and the Spanish feared the pressures that the new United States would bring upon their possessions in the New World. When France sent its first minister to the United States in the summer of 1778, he was warned by Vergennes that both the United States and Spain hoped to conquer the Floridas; he was instructed to prepare the Americans for the likelihood that they would have to forego expansion in that region.

Spain was anxious to win back lost possessions from England but did not want to encourage colonial separatist movements by recognizing American independence. The Spanish turned away all American overtures for a treaty. When Spain entered the war in the early summer of 1779, it was in alliance with France, not the United States, and with the hope of regaining from England her old possessions of Gibraltar, Minorca, and the Floridas. Spain failed to achieve its European objectives, but was successful in capturing British Mobile and Pensacola and in taking control of West Florida.

Realizing the inability of the United States to capture the Floridas, Congress had already in August 1779 sketched out possible peace terms that would leave the Floridas in British hands. In outlining terms for an acceptable peace, Congress insisted on independence, a western boundary on the Mississippi River, a southern boundary at the 31st parallel, and free navigation of the Mississippi River. Congress also decided that, while Canada was desirable and of great importance, peace would not depend on its cession. By the summer of 1779, the United States had to recognize the reality that the power to take Canada and the Floridas, much less Bermuda, was still beyond its reach.

American efforts to involve other European powers directly in its behalf were unsuccessful during the Revolution, although important financial aid was secured in the Netherlands, and other European countries became indirectly involved because of the widening scope of the conflict. To resist British maritime policies, a number of nations joined a League of Armed Neutrality, an organization to defend the commercial rights of neutrals in time of war. The provisions of the Armed Neutrality were similar to those of the American model treaty of 1776: free ships make free goods, the right to trade between the ports of a belligerent, a limited list of contraband, and an attempt to limit blockades. Armed Neutrality was declared by Catherine the Great of Russia early in 1780; she quickly gained the adherence of two other Baltic nations—Denmark and Sweden. The Netherlands, Prussia, Portugal, and the Kingdom of the Two Sicilies joined later. These countries were anxious to protect their commerce from harassment by the belligerents, but they were not anxious to throw their support to the United States in its struggle with England. Russia was unreceptive to American efforts to join the league, although the Armed Neutrality was an indirect help to the Americans because it hindered British maritime policies. Great Britain would not agree to neutral desires and, irritated by the manner in which Dutch trade aided British enemies, had formally declared war on the Netherlands before that country joined the Armed Neutrality.

American ability to deal with foreign nations increased somewhat in March 1781, when the Articles of Confederation went into effect. This attempt at forming a unified government signified to foreign powers the American determination to create a new nation. Under the articles, Congress was given the sole right of establishing peace and declaring war, of sending and receiving ambassadors, and of entering into treaties and alliances with foreign nations. The articles also stated that Canada could enter the union whenever it wanted to; other new admissions would require the approval of nine states. Congress now appointed a Secretary of Foreign Affairs, who was directly responsible to Congress; Robert R. Livingston of New York served as Secretary from 1781 to 1783, and John Jay of the same state from 1784 and 1789.

Even now, however, there was great difficulty in achieving prompt and effective action in foreign affairs. Under the articles, Congress was given neither the power to control commerce nor the power of direct taxation. This meant that it was extremely difficult to negotiate effective commercial treaties, and as lack of money made it impossible to raise effective military forces once the war had ended, the United States had no way of backing its diplomacy with power. Also, as

Congress needed a two-thirds vote for many decisions, discussion was slow and it was simple for factions to block effective action. While the Revolution was actually being fought, dire necessity often speeded decision-making in foreign affairs, but in the years from 1783 to 1789 Congress was to be inept in its conduct of foreign policy.

In June 1781, following the adoption of the Articles of Confederation, Congress decided to appoint a peace commission that could respond to any British indication that they were willing to negotiate American independence. In the previous year, when it had seemed possible that Spain might act as a mediator, John Adams had been appointed to negotiate for the United States. Now Franklin, Jay, Henry Laurens, and Thomas Jefferson were appointed to join Adams. American independence and sovereignty were to be included in any treaty, but the commissioners were allowed to use their discretion on all other questions. The problems of a long war and of obtaining easy cooperation from European powers had tempered the early optimism regarding what could be obtained in addition to independence. The commissioners were also instructed to act in concert with the French, to be quite candid in dealing with them, and to do nothing in negotiations with the British without French "knowledge and concurrence." These instructions were later to be ignored in order to secure more favorable terms than the French seemed willing to defend.

Prospects for a quick peace still appeared bleak in the summer of 1781, but suddenly, in the fall of the same year, the way was opened for American independence. In the summer of 1781 British General Charles Cornwallis had campaigned in Virginia, forcing Thomas Jefferson and the members of the legislature to flee from Charlottesville. In August he established a camp at Yorktown in an apparently safe position. There he was trapped, for French naval forces succeeded in cutting off his supplies from the sea while General Washington and a force of American and French troops besieged him on the land. In mid-October Cornwallis surrendered with his army of nearly eight thousand men. This catastrophe led to the collapse of the British government under Lord North. The new ministers immediately prepared to negotiate with the Americans. Great Britain could have continued to fight the Revolution, but the war was unpopular, expensive, and extremely difficult to win.

Preliminary peace talks began in Paris in April 1782. At that time Franklin was the only American commissioner present. Adams was in the Netherlands, where he succeeded in obtaining Dutch recognition of American independence, a loan, and a commercial treaty. Jay was in Spain, where he had no success. Formal peace negotiations began in Paris in September, with Franklin and Jay present. Adams arrived in the middle of the negotiations in late October; Laurens only arrived when most of the negotiations were finished. Jefferson came to Europe too late to play any part in the negotiations.

In Franklin's preliminary talks with British envoy Richard Oswald, he had asked not only for independence and a Mississippi boundary, but also for the cession of part of Canada. Great Britain resisted this request, but proved reasonably generous in its peace terms. This stemmed not only from a desire to get out of a long and expensive war, but also from the wish to woo the United States away from French influence. The American commercial connection was of great importance to the British, and they had no wish to drive the United States further into the arms of France. On their part, the French, having succeeded in breaking up the British empire, had no desire to enhance the power of the United States. To do this, particularly in the Mississippi Valley, would only serve to alienate France's ally Spain, and would make the Americans less dependent upon the French.

Although the British had begun talks with Franklin, the next and most important stage of the negotiations was carried out by John Jay. Like John Adams, New Yorker Jay combined intelligence with a rigidity of manner and a touchy vanity. He had spent a depressing time trying to further American interests at the Spanish court, and he proved less willing than Franklin to trust that these interests could best be served by working closely with the French. Deciding that the French were ready to sacrifice America's best interests, Jay bypassed Franklin and began separate negotiations with the British; in doing so he ignored both the alliance with France and the instructions from Congress. When, in the fall of 1782, John Adams arrived in Paris from the Netherlands, he gave his full support to Jay's actions. Franklin was less enthusiastic, but was persuaded to agree to the separate course of action.

The preliminary articles of peace between the United States and Great Britain were signed on November 30, 1782. France reacted less strongly than might have been expected, for Vergennes was able to use the American actions as an excuse for not fulfilling France's own obligations to Spain. In their treaty of alliance France had promised Spain not to make peace until Spain had regained Gibraltar from England. The conquest of Gibraltar was proving extremely difficult, and Vergennes could now use the separate peace signed by the United States as a reason for bringing a general end to the war.

The final peace treaty between the United States and Great Britain was signed in Paris on September 3, 1783. By the treaty the United States obtained independence from England; Great Britain retained Canada; and the United States–Canadian boundary was set approximately on the modern line from the Atlantic to the Mississippi River, dividing Maine and New Brunswick at the St. Croix River, and giving both countries access to the Great Lakes. Because of inadequate geographical knowledge, it was many years before the entire boundary was delineated in detail. On the west, the United States obtained the Mississippi River as a boundary. On the south, the boundary between the United States and Spanish possessions ran along the 31st parallel to the Appalachicola and St. Mary's Rivers to the sea; Spain, however, did not participate in this Anglo-American agreement. The Americans retained their fishing rights off Newfoundland and in the Gulf of St. Lawrence, and were permitted to dry and cure their fish on the unsettled shores of Nova Scotia, the Magdalen Islands, and Labrador. All debts from before the Revolution were to be honored by the citizens of each country, and Congress was to recommend to the individual states that

Loyalists should be given back their rights and property. It was also declared that the navigation of the Mississippi River from its source to the ocean should forever remain open to the subjects of Great Britain and the United States. But, as in the case of the southern boundary of the United States, Spain was not involved in this decision.

Apart from the achievement of independence, the major United States success in the treaty was the obtaining of land westward to the Mississippi River. Most of the vast area west of the Appalachians was still in the hands of the Native American tribes, some of which had fought in the Revolution alongside the British. They were ignored in the peace treaty. European powers transferred land and defined boundaries in the New World without regard for the Indian occupants. It was assumed that the European powers, or in this case the United States, would work out their own relationships with the aboriginal peoples who occupied land within their international borders. This was to cause grave embarrassments to the American government in the years following the war, for the United States did not have the power to impose its will upon the Indians—but the commissioners had achieved their immediate objective and provided for American expansion far beyond the settled areas of the original states.

While the British retention of Canada left the potential of constant friction along the borders of British and American territory, the Anglo-American agreement on a southern boundary at the 31st parallel and the unenforceable statement in the treaty that the subjects of both countries would have the right to the navigation of the Mississippi from its source to the ocean ensured future friction between the United States and Spain. Spain had conquered British West Florida during the war, and also had an effective influence well to the north of the 31st parallel. The separate peace treaty that Spain signed with Great Britain provided for the cession of the Floridas to Spain with no mention of a specific boundary. In the years after the war Spain was to claim land far to the north of the 31st parallel. The Spanish also ignored the British–United States agreement for the free navigation of the Mississippi River; Spain controlled both of the lower banks, New Orleans, and the mouth of the river.

During the Revolution, the Americans had expected the lure of their commerce to be their main strength in pursuing an effective foreign policy. In reality, far more important had been existing European rivalries, and a European desire to reduce the dominating power of Great Britain. Most European powers resented Britain's arrogant maritime policies, and France and Spain were eager to hurt Britain and regain lost possessions. To help the United States was to hurt England. Yet, once the United States was independent, neither France nor Spain had any interest in enhancing American power. France wanted a satellite, and Spain feared for its American possessions. In 1783 the French alliance meant little. For all practical purposes the United States was alone. To achieve its commercial and territorial objectives it would have to depend upon its own resources.

THE CONFEDERATION ERA

In the years from the establishment of American independence in 1783 to the putting into effect of the new American constitution in 1789, the American government was ineffective in foreign policy. At the heart of America's problems was federal weakness, particularly the lack of central power brought about by the inability to levy direct taxation and by individual state control over commerce. At the beginning of the Revolution, Americans had dreamed of increasing agricultural and commercial wealth by the opening of markets throughout Europe. They had also dreamed of an expanding republic in which a rapidly growing population would obtain ample land for its needs by pressing westward onto the rich lands of the Mississippi Valley, and in which security for the nation and access to markets for western farmers would be ensured by the acquisition of Canada to the north and the Floridas to the south.

In regard to both commercial and territorial expansion, the

years after 1783 were a disappointment to most Americans. Although agriculture was flourishing and there was a strong and growing merchant marine, for the most part American trade was still tied firmly to the British, and on British terms. Territorially, the situation was much worse. In the lands beyond the Appalachians there was chaos. Widespread Indian warfare slowed or even stopped the advance of American settlement, and, rather than the United States acquiring Canada and the Floridas, Great Britain and Spain kept military establishments on American territory in the Northwest and Southwest and negotiated with the Indians within the territorial boundaries of the United States.

The commercial situation of the 1780s was particularly galling to those Americans who had hoped that American trade was so valuable that European nations could be wooed simply by offering a commercial connection. The most pressing problem was with Great Britain. Although some in England had argued at the end of the war that it would be of mutual benefit if the new United States were admitted within the British commercial system, conservative elements won out. The United States was excluded from the British system, and no commercial treaty was signed to liberalize American trading rights within the British empire. While the British allowed American raw materials to be imported into Great Britain in American ships, the Americans could no longer carry on their lucrative trade to the British West Indies (at least officially), nor could they trade by sea with Canada. In addition, many Americans were disturbed by the continued American dependence upon imported British manufactured goods. Not only did this create an adverse balance of trade, it also disturbed those who wished to see the new American republic freed from British influence. Some felt that New World republicanism would be in jeopardy if the British were allowed to corrupt the new nation with their goods and their monarchical ideas.

To add to the frictions caused by the nature of the post-war commercial relationship, various detailed provisions of the peace treaty proved impossible to fulfill. Slaveowners were not compensated for slaves who had been carried off by the British; loyalists were mistreated by individual states; and British merchants complained that their pre-war debts were not being repaid. These specific problems simply compounded the major resentments produced by the nature of the commercial relationship, and by the British violation of American territory in the Old Northwest. Immediate solutions seemed unlikely, for the British government would not even agree to send a minister to the United States.

The dissatisfaction at post-war commercial relationships with Great Britain was compounded by American unhappiness at the failure to sign satisfactory commercial treaties with other European powers, particularly Spain. Great hope had been placed in the 1778 commercial treaty with France, but in the years after the war, trade with France did not expand to the degree expected, even though France opened a number of her ports in the West Indies to American ships in 1784. Congress considered commercial treaties to be of such importance that in the spring of 1784 Jefferson was appointed to serve with Franklin and Adams in negotiating such agreements. Congress wanted these treaties to be based on the model treaty of 1776, with the addition of even more generous treatment for neutral shipping in time of war. The commission had little success. To the existing treaties with France, the Netherlands (1782), and Sweden (1783), were added treaties with Prussia (1785), and Morocco (1787). This was poor compensation for the lack of treaties with England and Spain.

The treaty with Morocco only served to emphasize another embarrassing commercial problem for the new republic. The states of Algiers, Tripoli, Tunis, and Morocco, scattered along the North African coastline, had long profited from raiding unprotected shipping in the Mediterranean. In earlier times their corsairs had attacked coastal settlements as far away as England. They not only seized ships and cargoes, but also enslaved the captured crews and demanded ransom money. Even large European powers often found the payment of "protection" money was simpler than defending shipping in the Mediterranean. Having achieved independence, the United States no longer lay under British protection, and the impoverished, proud new republic had neither the means nor the desire to give payments to the Barbary pirates. Only Morocco agreed to a treaty. Algiers, Tripoli, and Tunis committed depredations on American shipping and enslaved American seamen. The problem with the Barbary pirates was not as basic as the problem of establishing favorable commercial relations with the major powers of Europe, but it served to highlight the weakness of the new government.

The inability of the United States to fulfill its commercial ambitions cast doubts on the ability of the country to reach the levels of prosperity that had been confidently expected at the beginning of the Revolution, but the crisis in the Mississippi Valley raised more fundamental questions about the ability of the new republic to survive. The policies pursued by Great Britain and Spain in that region after 1783 convinced the Americans that their worst fears about having these two powers on their frontiers had been completely justified.

In the years from 1783 to 1789, in spite of all the difficulties and dangers, American pioneers pressed on across the mountains into the Mississippi Valley. The major areas of settlement were in what are now the states of Kentucky and Tennessee. From the end of the Revolution to 1790, Kentucky's population increased from 12,000 to 73,677. Tennessee's population had reached 35,691 by the latter year and was to double in the next five years. Settlers were also beginning to move into western Pennsylvania, and the very daring were attempting to cross the Ohio River into what is now the state of Ohio.

The most pressing problem in the Mississippi Valley was the widespread Indian resistance to the advance of American settlement. The American government acted with arrogance toward the Indians in the years immediately following the Revolution, claiming lands westward to the Mississippi by right of conquest rather than buying the desired lands from the various tribes. The Native Americans knew that the advance of the pioneers meant the ruin of their existing way of life and the loss of their lands.

The basic cause of Indian resistance was their desire to defend these lands, but the American government put much of the blame on the British and the Spanish rather than on the land hunger of its own citizens. The British and Spanish, while not causing the Indian resistance, took advantage of it. In the years after the Revolution, the British in the Great Lakes region and the Spanish on the Gulf negotiated with the Indian tribes within American territory, supplied them, and encouraged them to resist the American advance.

At the end of the Revolution, the British were in possession of a line of posts south of the new United States-Canadian boundary from Lake Champlain to Mackinac. These posts, which included Niagara and Detroit, effectively commanded the water routes through the Lakes and permitted contact with Indian tribes in a vast hinterland to the south and west within American territory. The decision to stay in the posts at the end of the Revolution was taken by the British authorities in Canada. Governor Frederick Haldimand feared a power vacuum and an Indian uprising if the British withdrew before the Americans were capable of taking control, and he also heeded the wishes of the Canadian fur traders who used the posts to influence the Indians and to control the fur trade. When the British government in London considered the question of withdrawal, they decided to tie it to the question of the American debts owed to British merchants from before the Revolution, arguing to the Americans that they were staying in the posts because of the American failure to pay the debts. American protests were in vain, and throughout the 1780s the British garrisoned the posts, dealt with the Indians within American territory, and actively encouraged them to resist the advance of American settlers across the Ohio River.

Congress fretted about its impotency in the Old Northwest, but could do nothing effective about it. The movement of strong American military forces to the Ohio River would have changed the balance of power in the region, but this was quite beyond Congress's ability. The central government had only the means to support one regular regiment of infantry in the years after

1783; efforts to raise another had to be abandoned owing to the lack of money. What troops Congress had were used on the Ohio, but for the most part settlers had to depend on their own militia to resist Indian attacks. It was clearly in the interest of the Indian tribes to cooperate with the British, for while the Americans intended to dispossess the Indians and farm the land between the Ohio and the Mississippi, the British hoped to make it a fur trading preserve which would keep the Americans well to the south of British possessions on the Great Lakes.

Anger and anxiety caused by the British retention of Canada went far beyond concern at the British role in helping to stop the advance of the frontier. There was also considerable fear that British intrigue was being used to bring about the disintegration of the republic. Contemporary political theorists and politicians drew on those earlier writers from classical times to the mid-eighteenth century who had argued that republics were liable to collapse through a combination of internal intrigue and external pressure. The American leaders were particularly sensitive to this possibility of collapse because of the widespread belief that the only successful republics had been small. Many cited Montesquieu's argument that a republic could not long subsist except in a small territory. In the Revolution it has often been argued that the possession of Canada and Florida was essential for American security; after 1783 it was often argued that the failure to obtain those regions had produced the consequences that had been prophesied.

The British authorities in Canada fueled American suspicions by making contact with dissatisfied Americans both in Vermont and Kentucky. In the 1780s, Vermont was anxious to achieve separate statehood, and Kentucky had no safe outlet for its goods and was under constant Indian attack. With the American Congress unable to provide help or leadership, there was a temptation for the dissatisfied to toy with foreign connections. Some in Vermont looked to the British in Canada, and some in Kentucky looked to either the British or the Spanish. Throughout the 1780s, American leaders revealed their suspicions that Britain was intriguing with American citizens. Secretary of

Foreign Affairs John Jay was particularly wary of this. He believed that there were strong ties between Vermont and Canada, and he advanced the suspicion that Shay's Rebellion in Massachusetts in 1786 had been effected by the connivance of the British authorities in Canada. In 1788 the Governor of the Northwest Territory, Arthur St. Clair, reported that a British agent was said to be travelling to Kentucky to induce the people there to "throw themselves into the Arms of Great Britain."

For the Americans of the Confederation era, the perceived threat from Canada was only one wing of a threatened encirclement, for the Spanish possession of New Orleans and the Floridas presented immediate problems that affected more settlers than the British retention of the posts and encouragement of Indian resistance. Spain realized the threat posed to its North American possessions by the new American republic. During the Revolution, the Americans had frequently expressed their desire for the possession of the Floridas and for the free navigation of the Mississippi River. In the years following the war, the Spanish in the southwest did all they could to advance their own interests in the region from the Gulf coast to the Ohio River; supplying and allying with the Indians on the borders of the United States; sending warships up the Mississippi River; keeping agents and troops north of the 31st parallel; and intriguing with American settlers in Tennessee and Kentucky.

The American government was desperately keen to achieve a settlement with Spain in the years after 1783. The United States wanted a general treaty that would give its shipping an entry into the extensive Spanish possessions, the right of the free navigation of the Mississippi to the ocean, and a recognized boundary at the 31st parallel. Spain felt no need to yield on any of these demands, although it was willing to sign a commercial treaty if one could be shaped in such a way as to be favorable to Spain's interests. In the 1780s, the United States was trying to deal with the Spanish from a position of weakness. The Spanish recognized this, and saw no reason to yield to American objectives that were injurious to Spanish interests.

For the Mississippi Valley settlers, the most vital of all the outstanding problems with Spain was the right to ship goods through New Orleans to the Gulf. Without this right they had no market for a large part of their produce. In 1784, the Spanish decided to bring pressure to bear on the American settlements by closing the lower Mississippi to American traffic. This was a true crisis for the trans-Appalachian settlers, and Congress was in dire need of an arrangement with Spain.

The opportunity for negotiations was made possible in 1785 by the arrival in the United States of Spanish minister Diego de Gardoqui. Spain had authorized him to negotiate, and even to concede a 31st parallel boundary if he thought it necessary, but he was not to give the Americans the right of free navigation of the Mississippi. In negotiating for the United States, American Secretary of Foreign Affairs John Jay had been instructed by Congress that he could not concede any exclusive Spanish right to navigate the Mississippi. Jay found Gardoqui to be a skillful negotiator, who tried to play on Jay's vanity while paying flattering attention to Mrs. Jay. Jay's basic problem, however, was that Spain had no motive to satisfy the main American desires. The best that Jay could obtain was a draft treaty which provided for trade between the United States and European Spain. The United States was not to be allowed into the desirable trade of the Spanish possessions in South America, but what was even worse was that, in return for a limited trade agreement, Gardoqui insisted that the United States should give up the right to navigate the lower Mississippi for a thirty-year period.

Jay asked Congress for permission to modify his original instructions and caused an uproar. Most of the settlers in Kentucky and Tennessee had emigrated to those areas from Virginia and North Carolina, and the southern representatives in Congress now rallied behind their western compatriots and bitterly opposed a treaty which would sacrifice the economic interests of the westerners for thirty years. With southern opposition it was impossible for Jay to get the two-thirds vote that he would need for the ratification of any treaty, and the proposed treaty with Spain was abandoned. The westerners, however, were enraged when they discovered that Jay had proposed signing a treaty so hostile to their interests.

Jay's willingness to concede the navigation of the Mississippi to the Spanish revealed a dilemma in American thinking that increasingly arose to plague the Americans in the 1780s. Since the middle of the eighteenth century prophesies of a population expanding across the entire Mississippi Valley had become common, but on observing the chaos across the mountains in the 1780s, some easterners began to doubt whether the republic had the centralized power to expand westward indefinitely. While some continued to dream of a great nation encompassing much of the continent, others now feared the effects of too rapid an expansion beyond the mountains. To some it seemed likely that the existing weakness of the republic would be deepened by rapid western growth, and that, with the British in Canada and the Spanish in Louisiana and the Floridas, there was a strong likelihood that outlying areas would separate from the original states to form more profitable connections. Secretary of Foreign Affairs John Jay argued in 1786 that the westward advance should be more measured and cautious, and not so far-flung. He was inspired to think of this by the constant Indian troubles, that seemed incapable of solution, and also by his increasing fear that the Confederation government had not the means to protect the interests of its citizens. "When Government either from Defects in its Construction or Administration ceases to assert its Rights," he told John Adams in November 1786, "or is too feeble to afford Security, inspire Confidence and overawe the ambitious and licentious, the best Citizens naturally grow uneasy and look to other Systems."

The situation in the Southwest following the failure of the Jay-Gardoqui negotiations served to intensify the fears of those who saw the republic as threatened by internal weakness and foreign intrigue. Gardoqui now began to talk to Americans who had an interest in the Kentucky and Tennessee settlements, and suggested the advantages to those regions of having an allegiance to Spain rather than to the impotent United States.

Chief among these advantages would be the right to ship goods freely through New Orleans to the ocean. Some westerners took advantage of Spanish responsiveness and made their own arrangements to trade through New Orleans. In 1787, James Wilkinson, who was later to serve as a general in the United States army, travelled to New Orleans and was empowered to grant licenses for Kentuckians to export down the Mississippi. In return he swore his allegiance to the Spanish government.

By contacts with Wilkinson, and by additional contacts with Tennessee leaders, the Spanish became hopeful that they could persuade the western settlers to cast their lot with Spain. In the late 1780s, the Spanish allowed limited trade through New Orleans and continued to deal with American citizens in Tennessee and Kentucky. It seems likely that the Americans involved were simply hoping for economic advantages by dealing with the Spanish, but unless the United States government could devise a way to protect the interests of its trans-Appalachian settlers, the possibility of separation would continue. From the Great Lakes to the Gulf, Congress had little influence, and American settlers attempted to contend alone with Indian resistance and with British and Spanish intrigue.

From the mid-1780s, the conviction that the survival and the commercial and territorial expansion of the republic depended upon a reshaped government began to gain ground. The problem of conducting an effective foreign policy was only one ingredient in a complex of motives that eventually led to a new constitution, but it was an important one. It was not simply that many were disappointed with the inability of Congress to shape effective commercial agreements with Great Britain, Spain, or other powers, or that there was an obvious inability to defend American interests against either the Indian tribes or foreign powers in the Mississippi Valley, it was now strongly felt that the situation on the borders of the United States threatened the very security and survival of the republic.

The discussions in the second half of the 1780s led to the writing of a new constitution at Philadelphia in 1787, its ratification in the states in the following months, and the inauguration of a new government in 1789. In this period America's political leaders were forced to readdress the question of what posture the country should assume in regard to foreign nations, and whether the dream of world-wide markets and a constant expansion on the North American Continent was feasible for a republican nation.

At Philadelphia in 1787, the need for the United States to deal effectively with its foreign problems played a key role in how the Constitution was shaped. Of major concern to those who were pressing for a stronger national government were the questions of the control of foreign commerce and direct federal taxation. The former would permit commercial regulation as a political and diplomatic weapon, and the latter would make possible a military force that could attempt to solve America's pressing security problems in the Mississippi Valley. Those who were content with the concentration of power in the states argued that the country should be emphasizing the internal welfare of its citizens, not its external posture, but this was challenged by those who contended that the survival of the country depended on the control of internal disunity and external threats. Alexander Hamilton argued that no government could give tranquility and happiness at home "which did not possess sufficient stability and strength to make us respectable abroad."

The new constitution made possible for the first time a strong, centralized direction of foreign affairs. The new system of government for the first time gave the direction of foreign policy to a strong executive. Rather than a committee of Congress, as there had been during most of the Revolution, or a secretary responsible to Congress, as in the Confederation era, the Constitution made possible a Secretary of State appointed by and responsible to the President. Although the Senate was given the power to approve appointments and act on treaties, for which a two-thirds majority would be needed for approval, the President was given the power to make the treaties. The two-thirds rule was to make sure that agreements such as that proposed by Jay and Gardoqui could not be forced through by a simple majority against the wishes of a group of states. The day by day conduct of foreign affairs was now to be taken over by the executive branch of the government. The precise form this would take was not made clear until the first years of the new government. In 1789 the new Congress provided for a Secretary of State, but even then President Washington for a time believed that he might seek personal advice on foreign affairs from the Senate rather than simple treaty approval or disapproval. Quickly, however, it became apparent that the President would seek advice from his Secretary of State and, as the 1790s progressed, from an evolving cabinet that consisted of his main secretaries—State, Treasury, War, and the Attorney General.

The President was also given considerable discretion in foreign policy by his constitutional power as "Commander in Chief of the Army and Navy of the United States." Later in American history, this made it possible for the President to move troops or ships in such a manner as to precipitate crises that then needed Congressional action. Congress was given the power to declare war, but a declaration of war, unlike the approval of treaties, needed only a simple majority, in this case in both houses. Congress was also given the power to lay and collect taxes, and "to regulate Commerce with foreign Nations, and among the several States, and with the Indian Tribes."

The vigorous debate in 1787 and 1788 over the ratification of the new federal constitution involved in part a sharp discussion of whether the dreams of a nation spanning the Mississippi Valley or the continent were possible. At the heart of the argument was a discussion of the nature of republics. The opponents of the new constitution made much of those writers, particularly Montesquieu, who had argued that a republic could survive only if small. This was challenged by supporters of the new document, particularly by Alexander Hamilton and James Madison. Hamilton and Madison advanced many of their arguments in a series of separate articles, along with some by John Jay, written originally for newspaper publication, and subsequently gathered together as *The Federalist*. These articles demonstrated the extent to which Hamilton and Madison, who later differed sharply on the conduct of American foreign policy, agreed on aspects of national growth.

In Federalist Nos. 10 and 14, Madison directly challenged the idea that republics had to be small by arguing that those who stated that the republic could not be large had confused a republic with a democracy. In a democracy, argued Madison, the people met and exercised government in person; in a republic they sent representatives. In this way there was no problem with a republic of large and increasing size, for representation could be extended indefinitely. Madison argued that the very size of a representative republic would stop the factionalism which was so feared in the 1780s. In Federalist No. 9, Hamilton tried to refute those who had cited Montesquieu in favor of a small territory for republican governments by pointing out that Montesquieu had also argued that a 'confederate republic' was a means of extending the sphere of popular government. This Montesquieu had argued, "has all the internal advantages of a republican, together with the external force of a monarchical, government." Both Madison and Hamilton agreed that the tendency to faction in one part of a confederated republic could be quelled by the action of the other parts. A few years later, in his *Rights of Man,* Thomas Paine showed his usual gift for grasping the essence of the argument in a single phrase when he stated that "What Athens was in miniature, America will be in magnitude."

In Federalist No. 11, Hamilton clearly delineated the degree to which he believed that a strong union could be the instrument for national growth. He said that there had been most agreement on the commercial value of union. "Under a vigorous national government," he wrote, "the natural strength and resources of the country, directed to a common interest, would baffle all the combinations of European jealousy to restrain our growth." With a strong union the United States would be able to thrust out foreign influence, dictate the terms of connection with Europe, and enable the United States "to aim at an ascendant in the system of American affairs."

The course of events from 1783 to 1789 had brought considerable disillusionment and fear to those who had believed that separation from England would bring unprecedented commercial and territorial growth. In writing a new constitution, those who supported a stronger federal system hoped once again to set the nation on the right track. It was not a question of simply doing enough to ensure survival, for while on the one hand they feared the failure of the republic, on the other they dreamed of a mighty nation trading with the world, spanning the continent, and exercising a controlling influence in the affairs of the New World. At the end of the 1780s, after years of American semi-impotency in foreign affairs, geographer Jedediah Morse wrote "we cannot but anticipate the period, as not far distant, when the AMERICAN EMPIRE will comprehend millions of souls, west of the Mississippi." He was able to write this at a time when Great Britain still controlled the Great Lakes, the Spanish held the Gulf and the lower Mississippi, and American Indians were successfully checking American expansion at the Ohio River. The Americans never abandoned the dreams of a greater America that had inspired them on the eve of the Revolution, and in writing a new constitution they hoped to establish a stable republic capable of survival and to lay the basis for the growth in commerce and territory hoped for since the beginning of the Revolution.

TWO

The British
Connection

With the inauguration of the new government in early 1789, the United States at last had some of the means necessary for achieving its objectives in foreign policy. It soon became apparent, however, that the lack of effective military power severely limited its ability to sway the policies of European powers; that there was fundamental disagreement among American leaders as to the best methods of attaining American objectives; and that there were increasing divisions regarding what these objectives should be.

The calibre of early American leadership on foreign policy was very high. In the executive branch, President Washington leaned very heavily on the advice of his Secretary of the Treasury, Alexander Hamilton, and his Secretary of State, Thomas Jefferson. Although as Secretary of State Jefferson should have had the key role in foreign affairs, the degree to which Washington eventually found Hamilton's policies compatible with his own views meant that the Secretary of the Treasury played a vital role in shaping the basic structure of American foreign policy. Hamilton's views were opposed by Jefferson, and this produced sharp disagreements within the emerging Presidential cabinet. At the Congressional level, Washington and Hamilton were in large part able to shape the decisions regarding foreign policy, but here, as among the President's advisors, vocal disagreements were expressed with the general tenor of the new policies. The opposition centered around Jefferson's friend and ally, James Madison, who sharply diverged from Hamilton's views in the early 1790s.

The basic economic policies of the new administration were shaped by Hamilton, and his domestic financial program depended upon a specific alignment in foreign policy. Hamilton envisaged taking a nation that was underdeveloped and transforming it into a mighty commercial empire. His program of funding the national debt and assuming the state debts was to be financed with revenue coming largely from duties on the extensive imports of manufactured goods from Great Britain, and the commercial ties with that country would provide the credit that the United States so desperately needed for growth. This would not only lead to expanding exports and trade, but ultimately to the development of American manufacturing.

Hamilton believed that the only sensible foreign policy for the United States to pursue was that of friendship and close commercial ties with Great Britain. His ultimate aim was a powerful, independent commercial empire for the United States and a dominant role in the affairs of the western hemisphere, but he thought it essential to reach that goal by continuing and strengthening the British connection. Hamilton was cautious in his estimate of American power, although he had great hopes for the future. Flowery images of an American empire stretching endlessly westward across the continent had no attraction for Hamilton. He thought it essential that the United States should have the right to navigate the Mississippi and access to the Gulf, but his eyes were cast toward the sea, not the land. If Great Britain were alienated, then American revenues would dry up, trade would be sharply reduced, and credit would cease. Hamilton tried to shape the nation's foreign policy so that none of this would happen.

In the years after 1789, it quickly became apparent that Secretary of State Thomas Jefferson and his friend James Madison were far more optimistic than Hamilton about America's immediate ability to carve out an independent role. At the heart of Jefferson and Madison's thinking was the concept of an agrarian republic. Both of them believed that a sound republic needed to be built on a base of land-owning freemen, and that America's growing population should be given the necessary land by expansion westward across the continent. But these farmers also needed markets, and Jefferson and Madison both tried to shape policies that would expand foreign markets for American produce. Jefferson at times attacked the idea of commerce and a commercial nation, but he realized full well that his Arcadian dream of an isolated, agrarian America was impossible of realization, and he was prepared to defend the right of the United States to export its produce all over the world.

Jefferson and Madison differed most sharply from Hamilton on foreign policy in their attitudes toward Great Britain. They both believed that instead of fostering the British commercial connection, America should be striving to spread its commerce over a much broader area. They were infuriated that Britain refused to sign a commercial treaty and that Britain conducted trade with the United States on its own terms. They thought that England should be forced into more reasonable policies by American commercial discrimination and disregarded Hamilton's arguments that such discrimination might lead to a quarrel which would ruin the basis of American finances and destroy the prospects of American economic growth. For Hamilton, British imports were an economic and financial necessity; for Jefferson and Madison they were a sign of a continuing, demeaning dependence on Great Britain and a means by which republican virtue would be corrupted.

The quarrel which in the next five or six years was to lead to the emergence of opposing political parties began in the very first session of the first Congress in the summer of 1789. As Hamilton wished both to raise revenue and to encourage the growth of American shipping, he was in favor of Congressional action which put a tax of 50 cents per ton on foreign vessels coming into American ports, and imposed a tariff which was 10 percent higher on goods brought in foreign vessels. But Hamilton bitterly objected to Madison's proposal, which would have given more favorable tonnage and tariff duties to nations that had entered into commercial agreements with the United States. The particular object of this legislation was Great Britain. Madison wanted to reduce trade with England and encourage it with France and other countries, and he wanted to force the British to permit more liberal American trade within the British Empire.

Hamilton strongly opposed discriminatory legislation against Great Britain, threw his influence against it, and helped to bring about its defeat in the Senate. Thus, in the vital area of foreign commercial relations as in domestic financial matters, Hamilton's influence and the influence of his supporters decisively shaped American policies in the early years of the new nation. American trade with England flourished in these years, and Hamilton did all he could to promote it in spite of continued British restrictions on American commerce, the British occupation of the Northwest posts within American territory, and the other disagreements emanating from the 1783 treaty. He was helped in influencing Washington in the first year of the new government by the fact that Jefferson, who had been minister to France, did not arrive to take over his post as Secretary of State until March 1790.

By the time Jefferson was taking any major part in shaping

the policies of the new government, chances for a general rapprochement with Great Britain appeared reasonably good because of a sharp deterioration in the relations between Great Britain and Spain. Early in 1790, Washington had sent Gouverneur Morris, the American minister to France, to London to find out whether England wished to begin formal diplomatic relations and to negotiate to settle outstanding problems. At first the British were not particularly receptive to Morris's overtures, but they became somewhat more interested in America's grievances when a crisis erupted in Anglo- Spanish relations. In 1789, British interests had tried to establish a fur trading post in Nootka Sound on Vancouver Island on the far Northwest coast of North America. The Spanish sent an expedition and removed it. Great Britain heard of this in 1790, and for a time the incident seemed likely to produce war. The Governor in chief of Canada, Lord Dorchester, asked Major George Beckwith, a paid British agent in the United States, to discover whether the Americans might be receptive to a request for British troops to cross American territory to attack the Spanish in Louisiana. Such permission became unnecessary because Spain backed down and the crisis ended. The incident, however, gave Hamilton the chance to try to draw Great Britain and the United States closer together.

As the British agent in New York, Beckwith was very close to Hamilton. Hamilton assured Beckwith of American friendship for England, and did all he could to counteract Congressional talk of possible commercial discrimination against Great Britain. The American Secretary of the Treasury was indiscreet in the extent to which he tried to undercut the American attempts, in which both Gouverneur Morris in London and Jefferson in America were taking part, to convince the British that unless they changed their policies the United States might take steps to hinder British trade and move closer to France.

The possibility of meaningful negotiations moved another step forward in 1791 when the British sent George Hammond as their first minister to the United States. The British government had decided that the new and more efficient American government might be capable of retaliation against Great Britain or of drawing closer to France, and sent Hammond not to concede any British claims but rather to talk and delay any American action. Hamilton again went out of his way to establish a close relationship with the British representative, although Jefferson pressed Hammond on the outstanding difficulties between the two countries, particularly the continued British occupation of the Northwest posts. Hammond proved unwilling to make concessions, for the British were quite satisfied with their existing relationship with the United States.

Great Britain's unwillingness to enter into meaningful negotiations with the United States in the early 1790s was matched by Spain. Any hopes that the United States could reap advantages from an Anglo-Spanish war ended with the settlement of the Nootka Sound affair, and American attempts to negotiate in Madrid encountered frustrating delays. The intransigence of both Great Britain and Spain, combined with strong Indian resistance, meant that the Mississippi Valley continued to be a crisis area in the early years of the new American government. Great Britain and Spain continued to violate American sovereignty in that region; both powers had agents on American soil; both powers continued to encourage and supply the Indians who were resisting the advance of American settlers; and Spain continued to control the Mississippi River for her own purposes.

Faced by this intransigence, and limited in possible responses by Hamilton's insistence on friendly commercial relations with Great Britain, the United States government in the early 1790s attempted a military solution to settlement problems in the trans-Appalachian West. Unable to raise troops to fight both in the Northwest and the Southwest, the federal government concentrated on efforts to make possible the settlement of public lands beyond the Ohio River. In 1790 and 1791 expeditions were launched northward from the Ohio River into Indian country. These expeditions were signs of the energy of the new government, but they were launched without adequate preparations and were unsuccessful. In November 1791, Arthur St.

Clair, the governor of the Northwest Territory, suffered a disastrous defeat when his army was overwhelmed by an Indian attack. This great Indian victory encouraged resistance throughout the Ohio Valley, and made it essential that careful preparations should precede any further military efforts. In the meantime, the American government attempted to convince the Indians that in future all lands would be fairly purchased, and that Indian-white boundaries would be strictly maintained. The Indians were well aware that such promises meant little.

In the early 1790s, the new American government achieved internal respectability and a boost to American economic growth, but it encountered bitter frustration in foreign policy. Hamilton was reasonably satisfied because he thought he had set the American government on the correct course, but Jefferson, Madison, and their followers were maddened by what they considered to be subservience to England, and by the apparent American inability to open the lands of the Mississippi Valley to settlement. They were also convinced that Hamilton's financial policies and his close ties with England posed a threat to American republicanism.

EUROPEAN WAR AND NEUTRALITY

The divisions of foreign policy that beset America's leaders in the years following the adoption of the new constitution became much deeper as a result of the onset of widespread European war in 1793. Beginning in that year England and France were to be at war for most of the time until 1815. War between England and France produced a general maritime struggle that brought constant harassment of American commerce and repeated crises in American relationships with the European belligerents. A partial consolation for these new crises was that with England and Spain deeply involved in European conflict opportunities for the settlement of outstanding problems in the Mississippi Valley were much improved.

American relations with France had begun to change from

the time of the beginning of the French Revolution in 1789. The outbreak of the revolution was at first greeted with almost universal pleasure in the United States. It appeared that American ideas of liberty were spreading across the Atlantic to Europe. The near unanimity began to disappear as the Revolution became more extreme. The King and Queen were executed, the Terror began, the guillotine worked busily, many fled, and a Goddess of Reason reigned in Paris. Since becoming Secretary of the Treasury, Hamilton had based his whole system on close ties to Great Britain; by 1792-1793 he could argue that because of the extreme developments in France the French alliance should be ended.

Jefferson was not repelled by the extremism of the French Revolution. He considered that though there was violence and terror, in this case the end justified the means. Monarchy had been overthrown in France, republicanism had triumphed, and the cause of world liberty had been advanced. Jefferson and Madison saw no reason to abandon the French alliance. They had long wanted to encourage trade and friendship with France to counterbalance America's intimate ties and extensive trade with Great Britain. Now they had even more reason to encourage this shift in policy, for to move toward France would be to move toward fellow-republicans and away from British monarchical interests. What is ironic is that Jefferson, Madison, and the southern slaveowners who were among their strongest supporters saw nothing incongruous in supporting the right of bloody revolution in France while oppressing a different race at home.

By 1793, the most important powers with which the United States dealt were at war. The main antagonists were Great Britain and France, but Spain, confronted by revolutionary France, temporarily reversed her traditional stance and allied with Great Britain. The outbreak of war between Great Britain and France in February 1793 soon brought a major crisis in American foreign policy. The United States was still allied with France. France had the right to bring naval prizes into American ports and might expect American help in defending French

West Indian islands. Within the American cabinet, however, there was no support for the idea that the United States should side militarily with France in its conflict with Great Britain. Hamilton, of course, was bitterly opposed to any aid to the French. He believed that the French treaties should be suspended until the course of the Revolution was known. Jefferson wanted neutrality, but he also wanted the treaties with France to continue in force, and he advised President Washington to receive Edmond Genêt, the minister who was being sent by revolutionary France to the United States. Washington agreed to receive Genêt, but the neutrality proclamation he issued on April 22, 1793, suited Hamilton more than it suited Jefferson.

The proclamation emphasized that the United States would act in an "impartial" manner toward the belligerent powers. Many friends of France in the United States believed that a neutrality which leaned toward France would have been more appropriate. Also, both Jefferson and Madison were disturbed by Washington enhancing the power of the executive by taking upon himself the authority to issue the proclamation. They believed that as Congress had the power over a declaration of war, it should also have the power over a declaration of neutrality. Their arguments were to no avail. Washington had followed Hamilton's interpretation of the powers of the president.

While the cabinet was debating how to respond to the European war, French minister Genêt was receiving a tumultuous welcome as he travelled from his landing place in Charleston to Philadelphia. Genêt was a brilliant and confident young man who found it difficult to believe that the Americans were not prepared to throw themselves enthusiastically into the revolutionary cause he believed in. Popular feeling seemed clearly to be on the side of the French. Genêt had instructions to use the United States as a base for operations against the British, and his reception encourged him to believe that the United States intended to be an extremely friendly neutral. When Genêt arrived in Philadelphia, he was warmly received by Secretary of State Thomas Jefferson.

Thinking that the United States would cooperate with

belligerent France, as France had helped the United States from early in the Revolution, Genêt proceeded to try to use the United States to attack France's enemies. As Spain was allied with Great Britain, he hoped to organize expeditions against Louisiana and the Floridas. He commissioned revolutionary hero George Rogers Clark to attack New Orleans, and advertisements in the *Kentucky Gazette* asked for volunteers for an expedition against Spanish territory. Genêt also commissioned a dozen American ships as French privateers. These vessels sailed from American ports to attack British shipping, and brought the resulting prizes back into American ports to be sold by French consuls. While beginning war activities on American soil, Genêt was also pressing the American government to enforce against the British those parts of the Franco-American treaty of 1778 that defined neutral rights in wartime. In particular, he asked the Americans to defend the principle that free ships make free goods.

Disturbed at what appeared to be severe violations of his neutrality proclamation, Washington took steps to curb Genêt's activities. In August 1793, the government issued rules to govern the activities of belligerents on American soil; foreign nations were prohibited from recruiting volunteers or outfitting privateers within United States territory. Washington did, however, continue to allow the French to sell their maritime prizes in American ports, and in spite of the new rules, Genêt still managed to send another privateer to sea to raid British shipping. Hamilton had long been shocked by Genêt's activities, but for a time Jefferson was less eager to condemn all of the actions of the French minister. In August, however, even Jefferson was swung around to an anti-Genêt position. In that month Genêt, convinced that he had popular support in America, threatened that unless Washington would call a special session of Congress to decide whether Genêt or the American government had acted correctly, he would appeal directly to the people of the United States. At this the American government requested that Genêt should be recalled. Jefferson persuaded Washington, however, that this should not bring about any sharp change in Franco-

American relations. Genêt ultimately found it more to his advantage to stay in the United States as a private citizen, for his own party had lost power in France, and the Jacobins were ready to try him as an enemy of the French republic.

The Genêt affair had shown quite clearly that Washington's government was determined to be neutral in the European conflict, despite the Franco-American alliance of 1778. Yet, there were sharp disagreements in America, for Hamilton still wished to stay far closer to the British than did Jefferson and the other opponents of his policies. As a result of this difference, the divisions in American politics that had developed around the issue of Hamilton's financial system began to widen, and within the next two years the Washington administration ended its bipartisan character and became an administration of the new Federalist party. In December 1793, Jefferson, who had been unable to carry the same influence with Washington as Hamilton, resigned his position as Secretary of State. Jefferson always had ambivalent feelings about the holding of public office, and in this case he was happy to end his association with an administration that was becoming increasingly Hamiltonian in nature. In cooperation with Madison, Jefferson was now to exercise leadership in the rapidly developing opposition party; a party that had assumed the name Republican to emphasize the degree to which its members believed that the Hamiltonians were subverting republicanism and driving the American government toward monarchy.

While Genêt's plans to use the United States as a base of operations against Great Britain were a failure, France was not disturbed by the unwillingness of the United States to join in the war against Great Britain. The United States could provide more to France as a commercial neutral than as a military ally. At the beginning of the war, France threw open its colonial ports to American ships and hoped that the United States would be able to uphold the concept of neutral maritime rights which the young country had first expounded in the model treaty of 1776 and which had been incorporated in the Franco-American commercial treaty of 1778. Under the slogan of "free ships make free goods" France could hope that its goods would travel on American ships and that contraband would be very narrowly defined. In time of war, Great Britain had the naval power to inflict great damage on normal French trade, and France needed any help it could get from neutrals. For the Americans, the European war provided the opportunity to do what they had wanted to do since 1776—find larger and more varied export markets and increase their share of the carrying trade. With Europe at war the opportunities were many.

Any slim hope that either the French or the Americans might have had that the British would allow neutral shipping easily to evade British blockades of French trade soon disappeared. On June 8, 1793, a British Order in Council ordered the capture of neutral vessels carrying corn, flour, or meal to French ports. These cargoes and ships were not confiscated, but the ships were taken into British ports, and the neutrals were obliged to sell their cargoes there. On November 6, 1793, a more sweeping order was issued, in which the British ordered their ships to seize all vessels, including neutrals, carrying produce and goods from or to a French colony. This measure was harsher than traditional British policy toward neutrals, for before the Revolution Great Britain had promulgated the so-called Rule of 1756, by which it was declared that any trade closed to neutrals in time of peace could not be opened in time of war. This November order went beyond that because before the war France had allowed the United States to trade with a limited number of French ports in the West Indies. England was now closing that trade as well as neutral trade with areas that had been closed before the war.

The British also caused particular anger by the way in which they issued the November order regarding the French colonies. Neutrals were not notified of the new policy until British ships were in position to seize neutral vessels in the West Indies. With no warning, American vessels were highly vulnerable, and the British quickly captured some three hundred American ships trading with the West Indies. This extreme British policy was slightly modified by yet another order in January 1794. In that month British policy was changed to accord with the Rule of 1756, but at the same time British ships were ordered to capture all vessels carrying military or naval stores to French colonies. They were also to capture any ships sailing to a 'blockaded' colonial port.

The question of what constituted a 'blockade' was to plague Anglo-American relations throughout this era. The American position was that for a port or coast to be considered blockaded the blockading power had to maintain ships in its immediate vicinity to prevent neutral vessels entering. Great Britain and France at times went far beyond this; they instituted 'paper blockades' by which areas were declared blockaded and the blockading power simply stopped American ships far out at sea or even off the American coast to find out to which port they were bound, seizing them if they were bound for a 'blockaded' port.

The news that the British had seized hundreds of ships as a result of the November order reached Philadelphia in March 1794. It was received with widespread anger, and it put Hamilton's policy of close economic ties with England in jeopardy. The reaction in America was intensified because of news that the British were also acting in an aggressive manner across the Ohio River in the Old Northwest. Since the failure of American military expeditions in 1790 and 1791, the American government had given General Anthony Wayne the task of training an army for a successful expedition against the Indians while attempting to deflect Indian hostility by constant negotiation. During these years, the British had continued to occupy Detroit and Mackinac. From these posts, they supplied and encouraged the Indians within American territory.

With the outbreak of war in Europe, the British authorities in Canada began to act more overtly and with more vigor among the Indians in the expectation that the European war might soon involve Great Britain in conflict with the United States. Speaking to a delegation of Indians in February 1794, the Governor in chief of Canada, Lord Dorchester, said, regarding the United States, "I shall not be surprised if we are at war with them in the course of the present year; and if so, a Line must then be drawn by the Warriors.'' News of Dorchester's speech reached Philadelphia along with the news of wholesale British seizures in the West Indies, and produced immediate demands for firm action against Great Britain.

Even before the news of the extensive seizures in the West Indies and of Dorchester's speech reached Philadelphia, Hamilton's opponents had taken up the issue of commercial retaliation against Great Britain. Although the attempt to discriminate against Great Britain had failed in 1789, the Jeffersonians remained convinced that it was in the interest of the United States to end commercial dependence on that country. They also felt that the Hamilton-influenced policies of Washington's government since 1789 gave proof of the anti-republican effects of British influence. Increasingly, both Madison and Jefferson argued that the agrarian republic of the United States was being threatened by the influx of British ideas and British goods. With these, they believed, was coming British corruption to sap the vitals of the new nation. They contended that Hamilton's policies simply favored the commercial, moneyed interests, not America's farmers, who, they argued, needed republican virtue and stability at home and diversified markets abroad.

Shortly before leaving office in December 1793, Jefferson sent to Congress a report on the manner in which foreign countries treated American commerce. The main intent of the report was to present evidence to show that France dealt much more favorably with American trade than did Great Britain. The British West Indies were officially closed to American ships even though the United States allowed a massive import of British goods in British ships. Jefferson proposed that in order to retaliate against the British and increase trade with France, commercial discrimination should be practiced against Great Britain. In effect, Jefferson was advocating America's own Navigation Laws to alter the pattern of Anglo-American trade, and to shift American trade from its intimate ties with Great Britain.

In January 1794, Madison introduced in the House of Representatives resolutions to carry Jefferson's ideas into effect.

He wanted special duties on British ships and British goods, and argued that this would not only alter the unequal pattern of trade between the United States and Great Britain but that it would also curb the unhealthy affect that British goods and credit were having on American institutions. This was a direct challenge to Hamilton's whole system as it had developed since 1789. Hamilton rightly viewed this as an attempt to move the United States closer to France and further away from England, and it raised for him the frightening possibility that the United States might eventually find itself in the war on the French side. Writing anonymously in a newspaper article early in 1794, Hamilton argued that American commerce would be largely annihilated in such a war, and that agriculture would be deeply wounded. And as nine-tenths of the country's revenue came from commercial duties, the financial situation would be calamitous.

Although shipowners and merchants generally opposed any commercial struggle with England, and dreaded the possibility of war, southern plantation owners and farmers from other parts of the country listened favorably to the arguments emanating from Madison and Jefferson. Hamilton's supporters fought desperately in Congress to try to block the discriminatory legislation, and in February, Congress agreed to delay action until March. By that time the discussion in Congress became far more vehement because news arrived of wholesale British seizures in the West Indies and attempts by the Governor in chief of Canada to enlist Indians for future war. Thoughts of a simple, retaliatory commercial policy were cast aside as some Jeffersonians now called for open hostilities against Great Britain.

Although some talked and wrote as though war against England was a necessary retaliation against British aggression, the Republican leaders as well as the Federalists were faced with a dilemma. The Republicans generally favored moving closer to France, but actual war with England would involve an increased regular army, a navy, and additional taxes. These were all opposed by the Republicans as likely to increase the anti-republican tendencies that they feared had already developed in

America as a result of Hamilton's policies and British influence. In the years to come the Republican leadership continued to believe that the most effective weapon that could be used against Great Britain was the manipulation of American trade. Jefferson consistently believed, as had most American leaders in 1776, that Europe could best be coerced by American commercial weapons.

While the Federalist leadership wanted to avoid war with England at all costs, Washington and Hamilton had none of the theoretical opposition to increased military forces that was voiced by the Republican opposition. Early in 1794, they advanced proposals to increase American military forces because of the increased foreign dangers; these proposals were attacked by the Republicans. The most important measure that was approved passed not so much because of the increased dangers resulting from the Anglo-French war, but rather because of the harassment of American shipping by the Barbary pirates. The seizing of American ships in the Mediterranean and the enslavement of their crews had continued to infuriate Americans. In February 1794, the Federalists were able to use this feeling to force through, against considerable Republican opposition, a motion to authorize the construction of six frigates. This figure was later reduced to three, but for the first time since the Revolution the United States was to have a fighting navy.

JAY'S TREATY AND RAPPROCHEMENT WITH ENGLAND

While Congress debated motions designed to retaliate against Great Britain for its aggressions against American commerce, Hamilton and his supporters worked desperately to head off any confrontation with that country. In March, Federalist Senators and Hamilton urged Washington to send a special envoy to England to try to find a solution to Anglo-American difficulties. Washington agreed, and decided to send the Chief Justice of the Supreme Court, John Jay. Jay was a man with extensive diplomatic experience. He had served on the peace commission during the Revolution and as Secretary of Foreign Affairs from 1784 to 1789. While Jay prepared to leave for England, the Republicans continued to press retaliation against Great Britain in Congress. A nonintercourse bill failed by the casting vote of the Vice President in the Senate. In March, a one-month embargo had been placed on Amercian shipping to prevent further seizures. It was later renewed for a month, but then was allowed to expire because of its disruptions to American trade.

Although Jay's instructions were sent to him by Edmund Randolph, Jefferson's successor as Secretary of State, Hamilton played the most influential role in convincing Washingon what these instructions should be. Hamilton also prepared the British for what to expect. As in his discussions with Beckwith earlier in the decade, Hamilton was indiscreet in the information he supplied British Minister George Hammond. Although the United States had little power with which to coerce Great Britain, one possible means of winning concessions from that country might have been the threat of joining the Armed Neutrality which had been formed by Sweden and Denmark before Jay left for England. The United States was invited to join, and Great Britain had good reason for not wishing the United States to defend her neutral rights within such a group. In reality, Britain had nothing to fear, for the United States cabinet decided to avoid additional European entanglements by declining the invitation to join. At first this decision was not made public, but Hamilton privately assured Hammond that the United States would not join the Armed Neutrality. Hamilton was convinced that, at all costs, the United States should avoid estrangement from Great Britain. He saw no purpose in threatening that country with American hostility, for he believed that the United States could only lose by a quarrel with England.

Great Britain believed that the concession to the United States and other neutrals of the neutral rights they wished in time of war would be ruinous to Britain's war effort and to her position as the supreme maritime power. This was the major problem for Jay as a negotiator. In time of war, the Foreign

Office deferred to the Admiralty. The British considered that their dominating position in the world depended on naval strength, and that commercial warfare was an essential ingredient in fighting France. To allow the United States to trade freely would be to allow France to substitute American for French shipping and would defeat Britain's efforts to ruin French trade.

The other underlying problem for Jay was that Great Britain had not the slightest respect for American power. British ministers knew that the United States had a very weak regular army and was only just beginning to build a tiny navy. They wished to trade with the United States, but not at the expense of the war effort against France or by placing in jeopardy England's traditional maritime rights. They believed that the United States needed British friendship more than Britain needed that of the United States, and Hamilton agreed with them. He advised Washington accordingly. The main purpose of Jay's mission was to avoid war against, or any estrangement from, Great Britain. In essence, Washington's government was offering friendship and American trade in the hope of achieving some concessions from Great Britain to ease the existing tension.

The summer of 1794 was not a good time for Jay to be negotiating in London, for the war was going well for the British and they felt extremely confident. Also, the British were irritated by the actions of James Monroe, the new United States minister in France. Monroe was extremely pro-French, and his public avowals of friendship were an embarrassment to Jay in London. In negotiating with the British Foreign Minister, Lord Grenville, Jay did all the could to cement a friendship between the two countries. His approach well-reflected the desires of Hamilton and his party.

After a summer and fall of negotiation, the only major British concession in the treaty signed on November 19, 1794, was the British promise to withdraw from the Northwest posts by June 1, 1796. This was of major importance to the American government since it meant that the United States would at last have the boundaries in the Old Northwest it should have had after 1783, and that a major encouragement for Indian resistance would be removed. Indians would still be able to visit British posts north of the border, but they would have less reason to believe the assertions of British agents that the Old Northwest was to remain an Indian and British trading preserve. This idea of the Old Northwest as a buffer state between Canada and the United States had been advanced by British Minister George Hammond in Philadelphia in the early 1790s, and British Indian agents had encouraged the Indians to believe that they had British support in stopping the American settlers at the Ohio River.

Even without the British promise to withdraw from the posts, the balance of power between the Americans and the British-Indian alliance in the Old Northwest was changed decisively in August 1794 by Anthony Wayne's victory over the Indians of the region at the battle of Fallen Timbers. Even before learning of the British decision to withdraw from the posts, the Indians felt that they had been deserted, for in the days following the battle, the British authorities refused to give the Indians any overt help that might provoke incidents with the Americans. Wayne's victory led in the following year to the treaty of Greenville, by which the Indians of the Old Northwest were obliged to cede a large area of land north of the Ohio River. Wayne's victory and Jay's Treaty opened the Old Northwest to American settlement. In 1790, there had been only a few thousand settlers north of the Ohio River, by 1810 there were over a quarter of a million. In 1794 the new government had taken a major step toward gaining security on its northern borders.

In commercial matters Jay obtained one useful concession and another that was so weak that it was rejected by the Senate. The British agreed to allow American ships to trade to India, an area with which the United States was to establish a modest trade connection, but they agreed on only an extremely limited American admission into the vital area of the British West Indies. By the treaty which Jay signed, the British West Indies were opened to American vessels not larger than seventy tons. Moreover, there was to be no export from the United States of the main West Indian products—sugar, molasses, coffee, cocoa, or cotton. This modest opening of the West Indies was so restricted that the United States Senate rejected this part of the treaty. The only real commercial concession had been in India, and that was of very limited importance. The British officially banned American trade with their West Indian possessions throughout this period, although the need for supplies frequently obliged British West Indian governors to issue special proclamations allowing American ships into their ports.

Apart from the limited concessions in Jay's Treaty, the British agreed to compromise on a number of outstanding issues between the two countries. Joint commissions from the two countries were to decide what amount should be paid for British spoliations on American commerce; what was owing to British merchants in debts from before the Revolution; and what was the true location of the St. Croix River, which had been named in 1783 as the northeastern boundary between Canada and the United States.

In order to obtain the formal agreement, the limited British concessions, and ways to settle outstanding irritants between the two countries, Jay abandoned American neutral rights as they had been asserted since 1776. The British were unwilling to yield to the United States on questions of neutral wartime trading rights. Also omitted from the treaty was any reference to another British practice—impressment—which was to cause great bitterness throughout the Revolutionary and Napoleonic Wars. The British helped to man their navy by using press gangs to seize seamen wherever they could find them. Their normal hunting grounds were British merchant ships, and the bars and brothels of seaport towns in Great Britain. Once seized, these men often served on British warships until the war ended or they were dead. Conditions in the British navy were such that even without impressment there would have been extensive desertions. As it was, British seamen deserted in large numbers when given the opportunity. Many of these deserters eventually signed on to American merchants ships, where conditions were better.

The British were anxious to recover their deserters, and to dissuade others from deserting, because their ships were frequently undermanned. Since 1790 the British had often seized seamen from American ships in British ports; along with some genuine British deserters, Americans were thus impressed into the British service. The situation was complicated by the fact that the British maintained a doctrine of "inalienable allegiance." Anyone born in Great Britain was still liable for service in spite of emigration. The British did not try to apply this to those who had been in the United States since before the Revolution, but it meant that it was of no use for anyone who was seized to claim that they emigrated to America since 1783. Also, British captains who needed seamen were often happy to make mistakes and take seamen who were American-born. The British were suspicious of all "protections," which certified the place of birth and were carried by American seamen, because it was simple for deserters to obtain false protections in American ports. The Federalist administration had not instructed Jay to include the question of impressment in the treaty, but he raised the issue in London. The British would concede nothing. Many Americans felt that in impressment, as in their curbing of American trade, the British were riding roughshod over American rights. This issue became more serious after 1796, and particularly in the Napoleonic Wars after 1803, when the British began to impress seamen from American ships on the high seas.

It was clear that the omission of any acknowledgment of neutral trading rights in Jay's treaty would bring bitter attacks from Hamilton's opponents in the United States, and even greater anger was ensured by the fact that commercial provisions in the treaty ensured that the United States could not impose discriminatory duties against Great Britain for the next twelve years. Since 1789 Madison, Jefferson, and their supporters had argued that discriminatory duties were necessary to free American commerce from British domination. They now had to react to a treaty which not only allowed the British to define American neutral rights but also provided that the United States would not discriminate commercially against Great Britain.

The administration kept the terms of Jay's Treaty secret until the Senate could act upon it. The Senate approved it by the minimum two-thirds vote of 20 to 10 on June 24, 1795; most of the support was from the North, most of the opposition from the South. Within a few days the terms of the treaty became known to the general public, and there was a widespread public attack on what was viewed by many as knuckling under to the British. Jay was burned in effigy, and the Jeffersonians were beside themselves with anger. President Washington had some doubts about signing the treaty, particularly as he had news of further British seizures, but he signed in August. Even then the debate was not over, because the opposition made determined efforts in the House of Representatives to prevent money being voted to implement the detailed provisions of the treaty.

The 1795-1796 debate over Jay's Treaty cemented the party divisions that had begun to emerge earlier in the decade. By the end of these debates there was no doubt that Congress and the country were decisively divided into Federalist and Republican parties with divergent views on foreign as well as domestic policy. Although Hamilton resigned from the Washington administration early in 1795, he continued to influence policy, and Washington's administration was now decisively Federalist. Jefferson's successor as Secretary of State, Edmund Randolph of Virginia, resigned from the administration in the summer of 1795 when evidence was presented that he had been indiscreet in seeking help from the French minister in the United States. The leaders of both parties were convinced by 1795-1796 that members of the opposing party were consorting dangerously with a foreign power—in one case Great Britain, in the other France. To the Federalists, Jay's Treaty had saved the country from ruin; to the Republicans, it had completed the degradation of the Republic.

The greatest strength of Jay's Treaty, and of Federalist foreign policy toward England, was that it avoided war or commercial conflict and allowed American commerce to prosper. In practical terms, Jay's Treaty was a decided success. Taking advantage of the opportunities offered by the wars in Europe, American commerce increased dramatically between 1793 and 1801. The exports of American domestic produce almost doubled, but it was the carrying trade that was the source of the greatest wealth and the shipowners and commercial interests who benefited most from the rapprochement with Great Britain. Re-exports from the United States, mostly in trade with the West Indies, increased in value from little over $2 million in 1793 to over $46 million in 1801. If there had been a break with Great Britain, much of this trade would have been lost; and along with it would have gone the revenues derived from British goods entering the United States.

Yet, although United States self-interest was served by not trying to insist that Great Britain accept the American definition of neutral rights and by agreeing to a trade relationship which, at least on paper, excluded American shipping from some key British colonial markets, the national pride of many Americans was sorely hurt by Jay's Treaty. The United States once again appeared to be bobbing in the wake of the old revolutionary enemy, Great Britain. A concept of neutral rights that had been argued since 1776 had been ignored, and the absolute necessity of a tight commercial tie to Great Britain had been conceded. Republicans now feared that the corruption of the republic would proceed with speed. The Federalists discounted these arguments, and were content to rest their case on the obvious material advantages of a close commercial tie with England, even if this tie was largely on English terms.

A collateral benefit of policies that took the United States further away from France and closer to Great Britain was a satisfactory solution of the problems with Spain in the Southwest. In the dozen years after 1783, by far the most important issue in the Southwest remained the question of the right of Americans to ship their goods down the Mississippi River through Spanish territory to the sea. Spanish policy had varied in these years—often depending on the manner in which local Spanish authorities interpreted their instructions from Spain— but the increasing numbers of Americans dependent on trade down the river were extremely anxious that American rights should be formally acknowledged by the Spanish government. Although much American trade flowed down the Mississippi

River in the early 1790s, the trade was still dependent upon the whim of Spanish officials. Resentment against the Spanish was increased by extensive Indian attacks along the borders of Georgia and Tennessee in the ten years after the Revolution. It was well-known that many of the Indians involved were supplied and encouraged by the Spanish in the Floridas. To add to these practical problems the United States was still anxious to get a Spanish acknowledgment of the 31st parallel as the boundary between Spanish territory and the United States.

As a result of the French Revolution, the close royal family ties between France and Spain were severed, and Spain in 1793 had made an alliance with her old enemy, England. This alliance was threatened by 1794, for Spain was giving serious consideration to a withdrawal from the war and a separate peace with France. At such a time, when Spain could well fear the British reaction, Jay's mission to London caused considerable consternation in the Spanish capital. If the United States and Great Britain drew closer together, then Spain's possessions in the New World could be in jeopardy. In 1794–1795 Spain began to give serious consideration to an agreement with the United States regarding the outstanding problems on the Louisiana-Florida borders.

In November 1794, the United States minister to Great Britain, Thomas Pinckney, was ordered to undertake a special mission to Spain. He did not arrive there until June 1795. In the following month Spain signed a peace treaty with France. Spain was now ready to head off any Anglo-American agreement directed against Spain by signing a treaty with the United States. Such a treaty had been sought by the United States since the early years of the Revolution. The Spanish first proposed an alliance, which they hoped would include France, to guarantee all their existing possessions in the New World. Pinckney declined to commit the United States to such an alliance. The Federalists did not like the alliance they had with France, were anxious to avoid any non-commercial commitments with European powers, and had no desire to guarantee the Spanish territory along the Gulf, which they hoped one day to possess.

Anxious to forestall any United States-British action against Spanish territory in the New World, Spain now quickly conceded the immediate American objectives in the Southwest. By the treaty of San Lorenzo (also known as Pinckney's Treaty), which was signed on October 27, 1795, Spain agreed that the 31st parallel was the boundary between the two countries in the Southwest; that the United States could navigate the Mississippi River to its mouth; that for three years American citizens could deposit goods at New Orleans free of duty before shipping them elsewhere; that after three years this right of deposit would be renewed at New Orleans or at another spot on the lower Mississippi; and that each side would restrain the Indians within its territory from raiding across the border. Also included in the treaty was the old American definition of neutral rights—free ships make free goods; a narrow list of contraband; and a neutral right to trade with belligerents except in the case of strict, tightly enforced blockades. From the American point of view, all that was missing from the treaty was the much-desired right to trade with the Spanish empire. That Spain would not open this trade to American shipping in no way cast a shadow on the proceedings, and, in direct contrast to the partisan argument sparked by Jay's Treaty, unanimous approval by the United States Senate confirmed Pinckney's Treaty.

By the signing of treaties with Great Britain and Spain in 1794 and 1795, the Federalists could claim major diplomatic success on the North American Continent. The northern and southern borders had been secured, navigation of the Mississippi assured, and the trans-Appalachian West opened for settlement. The Indians had yet again been deserted—this time by the Spanish as well as by the British. In the Southwest there was no dramatic American victory to equal Wayne's success at Fallen Timbers, but the withdrawal of Spanish support, combined with the rapidly growing population of Kentucky and Tennessee, brought peace in the Southwest as well as in the Northwest. The settlers were now a much greater threat to the Indians than the Indians were to the settlers. Even the opposition Republicans could hardly quarrel with the diplomatic accomplishments of the Federalist government in the Mississippi Valley.

From the point of view of the Republicans, the weakness of Federalist policies was the continued dependence on close and what they believed were demeaning and dangerous ties with Great Britain, ties which were bringing about an increasing estrangement from France. This last problem was the major flaw in Federalist foreign policy; the French felt that they had been betrayed by the Federalist decision to sign a treaty with Great Britain.

THE COLLAPSE OF THE FRENCH ALLIANCE

Since 1793 and the rejection of Genêt by the American government, the French had good reason to fear the course of American foreign policy. The resignation of Jefferson from the position of Secretary of State in December 1793 was a severe blow, for Jefferson in these years could always be relied upon to temper any anti-French sentiment within the American cabinet. The French, however, could still feel that they had not been deserted, for Jefferson's successor, Edmund Randolph, was friendly toward them, and in the aftermath of the Genêt affair Washington sent the extremely pro-French James Monroe as minister to Paris. In 1794 and 1795, Monroe gave the French a false picture of the attitude of the American government. His sympathy for the French Revolution and the French government was in no way matched by the leaders of the administration he was serving.

The collapse of Franco-American relations proceeded rapidly after the signing of Jay's Treaty in November 1794. In Paris Monroe tried to assure the French that such a treaty would not be approved by the Senate, while from America French minister Jean Fauchet suggested to his superiors that an American agreement with Great Britain would require strong French action such as obtaining Louisiana from Spain so that the Americans could be compelled to follow a policy more agreeable to French desires. Fauchet's successor, Pierre Adet, threw himself vigorously into the task of trying to block Congressional approval of Jay's Treaty. In the summer of 1795, he made sure that its terms became public knowledge in the United States, and he encouraged Republicans in the House of Representatives to oppose the appropriation of money to carry its terms into effect. Well into 1796, Adet was still hoping that the American public could be persuaded to reject the treaty that their leaders had agreed to. He felt completely alienated from the American cabinet, for in the summer of 1795, Edmund Randolph had been forced to resign from his position as Secretary of State, and his successor, Timothy Pickering, was an uncompromising New England Federalist.

In 1796, Franco-American relations deteriorated to the point of collapse. In that year, Washington decided that Monroe was far too obviously pro-French and recalled him. Before he left France, the situation had worsened. France announced that she would treat American shipping in the same manner as Great Britain was treating it, and, on hearing the news of the final ratification of Jay's Treaty, informed Monroe that the United States had brought to an end the treaties of 1778, and that diplomatic relations would be broken off. In America, Adet had continued to be active in a manner that brought back memories of Genêt. He did not attempt to disguise his opposition to and dislike of the administration, and in the spring of 1796, tried to stir up the possibility of the secession of the region west of the Appalachians from the United States. By the summer of that year, the French placed what hopes they had of rapprochement in the possibility that Jefferson might win the Presidential election and bring about sharp changes in American foreign policy.

The French still believed that Washington was likely to continue as President, but he had decided to return to private life. In September 1796, he issued his Farewell Address to the American people. Washington originally wrote a draft of this address after reading a statement prepared several years earlier by Madison, but as it was eventually issued it depended a great deal on the ideas of Hamilton. After reading Washington's original proposed draft, Hamilton rewrote it, incorporating many of his own ideas. Washington also had suggestions from John Jay before deciding on the final form of his statement. Although the Farewell Address was to take its place in American history as a statement of permanent principles by the father of the country, its generalizations were very much Federalist generalizations intended to apply to the particular circumstances of the 1790s.

In the address, Washington dealt with both domestic and foreign affairs. It is not surprising that internally he warned against extreme party and sectional divisions, and against the dangers of foreign influence. This was very much aimed at the Republican opposition, and reflected his fears that the Republicans were too much committed to French ideals. In regard to foreign policy, Washington advanced ideas that had been current in American since the beginning of the Revolution, but these ideas were modified by the circumstances of the 1790s. Consistent in American thinking had been the idea that Europe had a set of interests distinct from those of America, and that America's ties with Europe should be commercial, not political: "The great rule of conduct for us in regard to foreign nations is, in extending our commercial relations to have with them as little *political* connection as possible." This had been the American contention in 1776—no alliances that brought commitments, simply commercial treaties. There is no doubt that Washington was thinking not only of the general principle but also of the specific problems with France in his statement that it was the "true policy" of the United States "to steer clear of permanent alliances with any portion of the foreign world." He emphasized, however, that the United States should not be unfaithful to existing engagements. What the United States should strive to effect were "temporary alliances for extraordinary emergencies."

The problem with Washington's Farewell Address as a permanent set of principles for American foreign policy was that it set up false hopes of the way in which the United States could pursue her commercial objectives abroad while keeping out of Europe's political quarrels. American exports and the American carrying trade were in 1796, and were to remain permanently, a vital ingredient in Europe's commerce. In times of general European war involving Great Britain and blockade and counterblockade, American shipping would always be a vital factor in the balance of power. Belligerent powers could not afford to allow the United States freedom of trade in time of war. Whether or not the United States had entangling political alliances was, and would be, immaterial. When there was commercial war in Europe, a belligerent would proceed against American trade if it thought it was of such value to the enemy that it could not be ignored. When this occurred, the United States would either have to accept disruption of its neutral commerce or be drawn into conflict, and, even if the administration was willing to suffer losses in order to trade and avoid war, public opinion would be stirred by what would be viewed as violations of America's neutral rights and injuries to the nation's honor. American efforts to continue her extensive trade with Europe in spite of European conflict were to take her into war in 1812 and in 1917, and were to cause her grave problems in Europe in 1940 and 1941 before Pearl Harbor. Since 1776, the United States has hoped to expand its commerce throughout Europe while avoiding political connections or quarrels; in time of general European war involving England and the whole continent of Europe, this simply has not been possible.

In the aftermath of the Farewell Address, the Federalists and the Republicans fought the first full-scale party election in American history. As the Federalist candidate, John Adams had the definite advantage of eight years' service as Washington's vice president. As the Republican candidate, Thomas Jefferson hoped to take advantage of the popular opposition to Jay's Treaty, and he contended that American republicanism was in danger from British influence on the Federalist administration. In making this attack, Jefferson himself was vulnerable to the charge that he was under French influence, particularly as French minister Adet, who was still in the United States, did all he could to influence the American electorate against the Federalists. Adams's narrow victory was a major disappointment to the French, and they now took stronger measures to show their displeasure at the pro-British policies of the United States.

In the winter of 1796–1797, French ships began to treat American vessels with the same lack of concern for neutral rights shown by the British in 1793. In March 1797 France announced that all neutral ships carrying any enemy goods would be liable to seizure. Relations between the United States and France continued to deteriorate throughout 1797, and the French expelled the newly appointed American minister to France, Charles Cotesworth Pinckney of South Carolina. The French were determined to force the Americans to acknowledge their grievances.

Adams's reaction to French anger was, at first, moderate. If at all possible, he wanted a settlement, and, as in the crisis with England in 1794, the Federalists decided to send a special mission in an attempt to solve outstanding grievances. In this effort, Adams had the support of Hamilton. The commission was a strong one: Charles Cotesworth Pinckney, John Marshall of Virginia, and Elbridge Gerry of Massachusetts. Pinckney and Marshall were Federalists, Gerry ostensibly independent, although he was to become a Republican. Their task was essentially the same as Jay's had been in England—to sign a treaty that would move the two nations toward peace rather than toward war. If possible, they were to obtain compensation for French spoliations of American commerce, and some modifications of the treaties signed in 1778; the United States very much wanted to withdraw from any responsibility to defend the French West Indies. In sending this commission to France, the Federalists demonstrated that though they were anxious to keep the friendship of Great Britain for commercial reasons, they had not the slightest desire to be dragged unnecessarily into the European war.

In general, in the 1790s, the Federalists wanted intimate commercial ties with Great Britain, neutrality in the European conflict, and enough military strength to convince the belligerents that the United States was serious in defending its interests. In 1797, as in 1794, the Federalists advocated increasing military strength as well as negotiation. In the spring of 1797, they proposed an increase in the army and navy and proposed increased taxation to pay for the new preparations. In 1797 as in 1794 the Republicans opposed military preparedness, arguing that such preparations were a threat to republicanism; as a result, the Federalists only achieved part of the preparations they wanted. At last the republic was beginning to create a fighting navy, for in 1797 were launched the three frigates provided for three years before.

The American commissioners met in Paris in October 1797. France was now ruled by the Directory, and much of the early republican enthusiasm had disappeared. France was in a transitional period between revolutionary fervor and the imperial ambitions of Napoleon. These were corrupt years, and the French leaders, angered that the United States had flouted the French alliance by signing Jay's Treaty, were in no mood for generosity. The French minister of foreign affairs, Talleyrand, would not receive the American commissioners, and after keeping them waiting for several weeks sent a number of intermediaries to see them in private. These intermediaries, later listed as X, Y, and Z in Adams' communication to Congress on this matter, suggested to the American commissioners that the path to negotiations would be easier if a bribe of $250,000 was paid to Talleyrand and the Directors, and if the French government was given a loan of $12 million. The American commissioners would not agree to this, but Talleyrand's agents later returned to press them to pay. At one point Pinckney replied "No, no, not a sixpence!" An American newspaper later changed this to "Millions for defense but not one cent for tribute." As such, the slogan became a rallying cry for American patriots.

Despairing of any solution, Pinckney and Marshall left Paris. Unwisely, Gerry decided he should stay to avoid a drift to war. He achieved nothing and had to leave in July 1798. By that time the news of what had happened in Paris had reached the United States and shocked Adams and his cabinet. In April

1798, the correspondence relating to the negotiations was published, and the X, Y, Z Affair brought immediate popular demands for retaliation against France. Responding to the popular outcry and to French intransigence, Adams and Congress now put the country on a war footing. By the early summer of 1798 a large increase was authorized in the new regular navy; public and private armed vessels were authorized to capture French armed vessels; commercial intercourse between the United States and France and French possessions was suspended; American merchant vessels were authorized to arm themselves and fight French armed vessels which attacked them; the treaties with France were abrogated; and an increase of the regular army to 13,000 men was authorized. Also, fearing the influence of the French within the United States, the government in June and July passed the Alien and Sedition Acts. These made it harder for aliens to be naturalized and easier for them to be deported, and provided for the prosecution of any Americans who wrote or published material attacking the government or its officers. The Alien and Sedition Acts were an indication of the degree to which Americans of this era believed that the republic was in danger from outside influence.

In spite of all the war measures of 1798, the Federalists did not declare war. This stemmed partially from the intensity of Republican opposition to such a step, but largely from the restraint which ultimately was exercised by John Adams. Adams, who in 1776 had first advanced the basic American strategy of extensive commercial intercourse with Europe but no political ties, was not of a character easily to be stampeded into any rash move. He was angered at the French in the spring and summer of 1798, talked of the likelihood of war, and pressed war preparations, but he was reluctant to take the final step. Adams wanted the United States free of the coat-tails of either England or France. Also, like any president of this post-revolutionary era, he was aware that the United States had pitifully weak military forces. Accordingly, the United States prepared to defend herself at sea, but did not declare war.

Even without a formal declaration, fighting began in 1798.

The three frigates launched in 1797 were ready for action in the summer of 1798. Although they could not contend with French ships-of-the-line, they were stronger than most French or British frigates and had far more fire power than any French privateer. These frigates were augmented by an increased and better organized fighting force, for in April 1798 Congress had established a separate Navy Department and in July had voted for further increases in the navy. To add to the American response, French armed vessels were also to be challenged by hundreds of privateers; private vessels licensed by the government to take prizes of French ships. This was a strictly controlled response, for American ships did not attack French merchant vessels. They did, however, make prizes of French armed vessels.

Congress also debated the necessity of raising an additional army of 10,000 men, and a provisional army of 50,000 men. These forces were never actually raised in these numbers, but Washington agreed that, if necessary, he would come out of retirement to take command. He insisted, however, that his second-in-command would be Alexander Hamilton. Washington was thinking of defending the nation against any French invasion, but Hamilton had dreams of a joint Anglo-American attack on Louisiana, the Floridas, and even other parts of the Spanish empire in the New World. From Hamilton's point of view this would have had the advantage of close cooperation with Great Britain and the opening of rich commercial opportunities in Latin America. Whenever in the years from 1775 to 1815 the United States shaped her strategy for war, major consideration was given to the acquisition of additional territory in the New World. At this time, however, Hamilton's ambitious dreams came to nothing. Great Britain was reluctant to back the United States in any endeavors that might help the United States more than Great Britain, and as the crisis with France progressed, President Adams became more and more suspicious of Hamilton's ambitions. Adams had ample reason to doubt Hamilton's full backing, for Hamilton had worked against him within the Federalist party in the election of 1796 and since then had frequently undermined Adams's position in his own cabinet and in Congress. Adams did not relish having Hamilton use the French crisis to enhance his own position and diminish that of Adams.

Adams's feeling that the French crisis should be eased not worsened was also increased by his realization that American commerce was being hurt by the naval war with France. The settlement with England by Jay's Treaty had been of great benefit to American commerce, for the British now acted with more moderation toward American neutral commerce. Although they continued to make seizures and impress seamen, they condoned much American trade that could have been considered illegal. American shippers developed an extensive trade with the French West Indies by means of the "broken voyage"; American ships brought French colonial produce into American ports before sending it to Europe and similarly took goods through American ports when trading from France to her colonies. The maritime war with France meant that the extensive carrying trade made possible by the war was now jeopardized.

The French also had little to gain from maritime war with the United States. In contending with British seapower, the French needed all the neutral help that they could get. France reaped great benefits from the neutral American carrying trade. It made little sense for the French to alienate the most important commercial neutral, however angered the French were by the United States rapprochement with Great Britain. It is not surprising that in the fall of 1798 the French began to give indications that they were willing to talk. Talleyrand had decided that this naval war was not to France's advantage. He let it be known to William Vans Murray, the American minister in the Netherlands, that he would be receptive to an American overture. The French even received kindly the American Quaker George Logan, who in 1798 travelled to France privately to try to seek peace. On his return in 1799 the Federalists pressed for and obtained the Logan Act which provided for the prosecution of private citizens who dealt with foreign governments regarding official matters concerning the United States.

Adams was willing to respond to France, although it meant

alienating some of his own party. In February 1799, he nominated William Vans Murray as minister to France. This was welcomed by the Republicans, but opposed by some of the more bellicose Federalist Senators and by Hamilton. Hamilton used all his influence against Adams's plan to deal with the French in Paris, but Adams was finally able to persuade the Senate that if they would not send Vans Murray alone, then a commission of three would be appropriate. Along with Murray, Adams nominated Oliver Ellsworth, who was chief justice of the Supreme Court, and William R. Davie of North Carolina. Although the Federalists were still somewhat divided, this commission was approved and travelled to France to try to bring an end to the unproductive naval war.

By their instructions the envoys were ordered to secure a large amount in reparations for French spoliations of American commerce, and France was also to be asked to accept the unilateral American ending of the Franco-American treaties of 1778. The French, who felt that they had been betrayed by the Federalist policy of friendship with Great Britain, were little inclined to accept both American demands. Although they now wanted to end the maritime war, they felt no need to bow to the demands of a weak national state. France was becoming stronger in the late 1790s. The Directory had been succeeded by the Consulate, and Napoleon was the First Consul.

The French response to the American demands was that the Americans could not have both the reparations and a French acceptance of the American abrogation of the Franco-American treaties. The French were adamant, and the American envoys decided that they would accept what treaty they could get. The Treaty of Mortefontaine (usually known as the Convention of 1800), which was signed on September 30, 1800, suspended the old treaties and ignored the spoliation claims, but it was agreed that these would be the subject of future negotiations. Most-favored commercial relations were renewed, and the treaty included the neutral rights principles of the model treaty of 1776, which had been incorporated into the Franco-American treaty of 1778. As the United States had abandoned these assertions in Jay's Treaty, it was difficult to see how the provisions of the French treaty were in accord with American policy since 1794. At best it could be said that these were the neutral rights that the United States ideally wished to maintain. As it turned out, the renewed assertion of American neutral rights was soon to have more meaning when the Federalists were succeeded by the Republicans in 1801.

The Federalist Senators quibbled at the treaty when it arrived in the United States. They disliked the provision which called for future negotiations regarding spoliations and the Franco-American alliance, and at first rejected the agreement. Adams asked France to accept the changes, and Napoleon did so on the understanding that no more would be said about spoliations. Not until 1801 was the treaty finally ratified.

The United States had now abandoned an alliance which it had originally signed as the only means by which it could gain French aid in the Revolution. In the years after 1783 the alliance had been more an embarrassment than an advantage, for there was a general agreement among American leaders that, while commercial connections with Europe should be encouraged, any political commitments should be avoided. In the 1790s, with an American government inspired by the ideas of Hamilton, the French alliance became an anachronism. Hamilton would have liked to see it disappear in 1793, when Revolutionary France and Great Britain began their long war. Ironically, the alliance finally ended in 1801 as the Federalists lost office.

The election of 1800 once again pitted John Adams against Thomas Jefferson. The presidential race was a close one, but Jefferson was able to use his southern base and his alliance with Aaron Burr in New York to forge a Republican victory. The Congressional results better reflected the marked swing in popular sentiment; the Republicans won a clear majority in the House of Representatives and were able to control the Senate with the vote of Vice-President Aaron Burr. The Federalists had shaped a sound central government, and they had succeeded in solving the outstanding problems with Great Britain and Spain in the Mississippi Valley. But the rapprochement with Great

Britain had been gained at a cost. On the one hand, the Federalists had been obliged to de-emphasize the American concept of neutral rights argued since 1776; on the other, they had been obliged to neglect their old ally, France, while ensuring friendship with a commercial partner, Great Britain. This had driven the French into a position of hostility, and the ensuing naval war had harmed American commerce. As a result of this conflict, even some New England seacoast towns gave a majority to the Republicans. The Alien and Sedition Acts played into the hands of the Republicans who argued that this showed quite clearly that the Federalists were prepared to change the nature of the republic.

Beyond all practical considerations, the Republicans were also helped in gaining office by the manner in which the Federalists, while winning material success, had been prepared to compromise on questions of national honor and national pride. The United States was still riding in the wake of the British man-of-war, and regardless of all practical considerations this was hated by those who better remembered Great Britain as the colonial overlord and the enemy of the Revolution than as the post-Revolutionary trading partner and supplier of credit. After 1800, with the Republicans in power, immediate practical considerations were sometimes to take second place to dreams of widening commercial opportunities and to anger produced by affronted national pride.

THREE

Retaliation and War

Jefferson's assumption of the Presidency in 1801 was to bring marked changes in American foreign policy. While both Jefferson and Hamilton agreed on the need for a prosperous, independent America, they differed sharply regarding its nature and how it could be attained. Hamilton believed strongly that the United States should shape its foreign policies to conform to the existing power structure of the post-Revolutionary world. As a weak but potentially powerful nation, the United States should recognize that the economic benefits of close ties with Great Britain combined with respectable military forces would provide the best route to an independent United States in control of the destiny of the Americas. British trade and British credit would enable American commerce to prosper and would ultimately allow the development of American manufacturing to complement other American resources. In the Mississippi Valley, Hamilton was most interested in security and in securing commercial outlets on the Gulf.

Jefferson's image of the future prosperity of the United States and how it could be attained differed in a number of important ways from that of Hamilton and the Federalists. Jefferson and the Republicans placed greater confidence in the contemporary power and influence of the United States than Hamilton. Along with his Secretary of State, James Madison, Jefferson believed that the American nation already had the inner strength and agricultural wealth to chart a strongly independent course. Jefferson and Madison wanted the United States to be a great and expanding agrarian republic; a republic that through its example would spread republican progress throughout the world. Jefferson believed that a virtuous, stable republic must, of necessity, be a nation of farmers owning their own land. He very much wanted to shield these farmers and the whole nation from all influences that would corrupt them. He particularly feared the extensive English imports that along with habits of luxury would bring anti-republican ideas. The ideal situation, which Jefferson realized was impossible of attainment and never sought, was an America isolated from Europe. "Were I to indulge my own theory," he wrote of the American states in 1785, "I should wish them to practice neither commerce nor navigation, but to stand, with respect to Europe precisely on the footing of China. We should thus avoid wars, and all our citizens would be husbandmen." In the years immediately after the Revolution, Jefferson gave much thought to this ideal. In his *Notes on the State of Virginia* he argued that farmers were the most valuable citizens, and that to remove the United States as much as possible from the chance of war it might be best "to abandon the ocean altogether." Other peoples could fetch and carry, and the United States would avoid the manufacturing that corrupted morals and endangered the republic.

Jefferson knew that his dream of a separate, isolated America was impossible. Both in his *Notes on the State of Virginia* and elsewhere he wrote of the interest of the American people in overseas trade. "Our people are decided in the opinion that it is necessary for us to take a share in the occupation of the ocean," he wrote to John Jay in 1785, "and their established habits induce them to require that the sea be kept open to them." With considerable foresight, Jefferson prophesied that this would lead to frequent wars. Jefferson realized that the farmers who formed the basis of his ideal nation needed markets for their surplus produce. The Republicans believed that the United States could use its trade as a weapon to open the oceans of the world both in peace and war. They thought that America's markets could be expanded, and they did not believe that America's prosperity and growth depended on close ties with Great Britain.

The Republican desire to sell farm produce abroad was combined with a surging nationalism that demanded a strong defense of American neutral rights in time of European war. The corrupt old enemy, Great Britain, should neither take the lion's share of American trade in time of peace nor should it tell the United States how to trade in time of war. Ignored was the practical reality that there was no immediate substitute available for the extensive trade with Great Britain, and that in time of general European war there was no way that the United States could trade without restraint.

Although Jefferson in the early 1790s had supported a policy that favored France rather than England, he realized by the time that he became president that his dreams of a new republican France sharing his own ideals had been frustrated. He conceived of Great Britain as the greater threat because of its intimate commercial ties with the United States and because of Great Britain's extensive naval power, but as Napoleon assumed power in France, Jefferson became increasingly disillusioned with a Europe that failed to share America's progress. The developments in France deepened Jefferson's belief that the United States had to make its own way in the world. After 1803, as Europe engaged in bloody war, and British sea power was pitted indirectly against Napoleon's mighty armies, Jefferson increasingly came to believe, as he had stated in his inaugural address in 1801, that the American government was "the world's best hope."

Abroad, the Republicans looked to breaking the close commercial ties with Great Britain, seeking other markets, and vigorously protecting American neutral rights in time of war. In North America they envisaged a surging expansion that would remove any last doubts about security on the continent while providing the agrarian base for a republic growing rapidly in population. "Our confederacy," Jefferson wrote in 1786, "must be viewed as the nest from which all America, North and South is to be peopled." He expanded on this idea in 1801, suggesting that the northern, and possibly the southern, continent would be covered by a population speaking the same language, and governed in a similar manner. He thought that problems of distance would preclude a single nation across the entire continent, but he believed firmly that expansion would produce sister agrarian republics. When the fur trading post of Astoria was established at the mouth of the Columbia River on the Pacific, Jefferson said that it was "the germ of a great, free and independent empire on that side of our continent, and that liberty and self-government spreading from that as well as this side, will ensure their complete establishment over the whole."

In the 1790s, Jefferson came to agree fully with Madison's contention that republics were best suited to large not small areas, and attacked Montesquieu for his contention that republics should be small. Like practically all other American leaders, including Hamilton, Jefferson thought it essential that the United States should have free access to the rivers running into the Gulf of Mexico, but he went much beyond this and disagreed sharply with most Federalists in his belief that rapid westward expansion was desirable to obtain ever-increasing areas of land. Jefferson justified his Indian policy with the argument that the Indians could be assimilated within American society, but its practical result was to transfer lands with great rapidity into the hands of the American frontiersmen. Jefferson avidly sought the lands westward to the Mississippi, and cast longing eyes on the vast areas beyond that river. He also continued to hold the belief, held almost universally by the American leaders of the revolutionary generation, that for the future security of the United States it was necessary to acquire Canada. In 1813, hopeful that Canada might be taken in the ongoing war, he argued that then the United States might insist in the peace negotiations "on retaining all westward of the meridian of Lake Huron, or of Ontario, or of Montreal . . . as an indemnification for the past and security for the future." Jefferson might dream of an ideal world in which the United States could cut itself off from Europe, but in that ideal world American settlers would be dominating both American continents.

In the first years of Jefferson's presidency, he was remarkably lucky in foreign policy. For nearly two years, he did not have to concern himself with the problems of neutral rights that had dominated the period from 1793 to 1801. In the fall of 1801, England and France agreed to a truce which was changed into a formal peace by the treaty of Amiens in March 1802. This was to provide only a brief breathing space for American diplomats, but it meant that in the first years of his presidency Jefferson did not have to cope with the dangerous crises at sea that had plagued his predecessors.

Ironically, while temporarily free of the insoluble problems posed by large-scale Anglo-French war, Jefferson was obliged to help direct a naval war of the type he had prophesied happening if American shipping roamed the seas of the world. The problem of the Barbary Pirates had never been solved in the years since 1783. The corsairs of Algiers, Tripoli, and Tunis sporadically raided American commerce and enslaved American seamen in North African ports. The new republic had neither the means nor the inclination to maintain a squadron in the Mediterranean to defend American shipping, but it also bitterly resented paying protection money in the manner that had become customary in Europe. In the mid-1790s, the Federalists talked of resistance but were prepared to negotiate. In 1794, Congress accepted the President's recommendation that frigates be built to be used against the Barbary Pirates. In reality, although conditions in the Mediterranean helped convince Congress that a navy was necessary, the Barbary situation was not the sole reason the Federalists wished to build a navy, and though the frigates were launched in 1797, the Quasi-War with France became a far more pressing problem than the Barbary Pirates. While the administration used the Barbary situation to obtain a navy, actual policy in the Mediterranean followed traditional European lines. In the years following the navy vote, the United States signed treaties with Algiers, Tripoli, and Tunis which cost the United States over a million dollars and which provided for future monetary payments to the Barbary states. Even this did not achieve the desired results, and from time to time American ships and seamen were seized.

Signs of more severe future trouble became obvious in 1800 when the Dey of Algiers forced an American frigate, which was bringing money provided for by the United States-Algiers treaty, to take gifts to Constantinople. The Dey was treating the United States as a tributary state. Disturbed by the frequent incidents, Jefferson on coming into office in 1801 sent four ships to make a show of force in the Mediterranean. Before this squadron arrived, a more serious situation had developed, for in May 1801 the Pasha of Tripoli declared war on the United States. He intended it to be open season on American ships.

Clearly in this case the new Republican administration had little choice but to provide the necessary warships for the Mediterranean, but the situation was particularly galling to Jefferson and his followers. Though they had a deep conviction that the honor of the republic should be preserved, trade protected, and injustice righted, they also intensely disliked bolstering the American military forces, particularly the navy. Jefferson had announced a policy of strict economy in government, and both he and his Secretary of the Treasury Albert Gallatin agreed that one of the best places to save money was by reducing the army and navy. For Jefferson this was not only the practice of sound economy, it was also a means of ensuring the subordination of the military to the civil authorities. Such subordination would preserve the republic from militarism and a possible threat to liberty. The navy was a particular target of the Republicans, for it enhanced the power of the Federalist commercial interests.

But, regardless of philosophical objections to bolstering the military forces, Jefferson had no choice but to carry on the war against Tripoli. The general American strategy in the war was to achieve a satisfactory peace by blockading the port of Tripoli. The few ships sent in 1801 proved unequal to the task, and further reinforcements were sent in 1802 and 1803. The United States suffered a major embarrassment in 1803 when the frigate *Philadelphia* ran aground and its crew of over three hundred were captured by the Tripolitans. Lieutenant Stephen Decatur led a daring raid to burn the ship before it could be used against the Americans, but a daring exploit which resulted in the American destruction of an American frigate could hardly be claimed as a major victory. In 1804, still more ships were sent to the Mediterranean, and in the same year, the American consul in Tunis, William Eaton, organized an overland expedition from Egypt to invade Tripoli. His army consisted of a handful of American marines and a motley force of mercenaries. The army took a Tripolitan town, and the Pasha of Tripoli agreed to a peace which was approved by the American naval commander, Commodore Samuel Barron. Eaton was annoyed, believing that his invasion could have forced a better peace from the Pasha. Barron, however, was worried about what might happen to the crew of the *Philadelphia*. The treaty of 1805 provided that $60,000 would be paid as ransom for the captured Americans, and that gifts would be given when a new consul was appointed. It was hardly a striking victory, but by 1805, the increasing dangers of the general European war made the United States little inclined to carry on a long drawn-out naval struggle in the Mediterranean.

The treaty of 1805 did not end America's problems with the Barbary Pirates. After American warships were withdrawn in 1807, more merchant ships were captured by Algerian corsairs. The problem was not brought to an end until 1815. In that year the United States sent naval forces to the Mediterranean to enforce a quick and favorable peace, with the payment of $10,000 by Algiers. Any chance of Algiers recovering after the departure of the American warships came to an end in the same year when a combined Anglo-Dutch fleet bombarded Algiers and destroyed its fleet.

The Tripolitan War should have demonstrated to Jefferson that, regardless of a desire to avoid warfare, a nation that was expanding on land and sending its commerce all over the world would encounter difficulties that would need the presence of an efficient military force, but he persisted in his hope that he could reduce his military forces while pursuing an expansionist foreign policy. Jefferson continued to believe that all nations desired American trade and that an extension of American republicanism was an extension of the area of freedom. He could not conceive that his revolutionary republican nation could have objectives that might clash with the best interests of other peoples. Jefferson believed profoundly that what was good for America was good for the world. Thus, in the years after the Tripolitan War, when the Republicans pursued a vigorous defense of neutral rights, they maintained only a weak navy. Arguing that the United States would never wish to wage offensive war, Jefferson concentrated his naval policy on a strategy of stockpiling shallow-draft gunboats suitable, he believed, to protect America's coasts from invasion. Even after 1807, when the crisis with England produced a modest attempt to strengthen the army, the Republicans continued to oppose any attempt to create a strong, fighting navy.

LOUISIANA PURCHASE AND THE FLORIDAS

The Tripolitan War was forced upon Jefferson. Far closer to his heart and to his deepest concept of America's interests was the crisis that developed in the Mississippi Valley in the first years of his presidency. The crisis enabled Jefferson to provide for the unlimited westward expansion that he believed essential for the future tranquillity of the United States. It developed because of renewed French ambitions in the Mississippi Valley. In the second half of the 1790s, various French ministers had toyed with the idea of renewing the French North American empire lost to the British in 1763. This idea was intimately tied to French policy in the West Indies, for it was hoped that a colony on the mainland could supply the necessary provisions for the French sugar islands. The old French region of Louisiana, now in the possession of Spain, seemed the obvious choice, for, unlike the British in Canada, the Spanish were vulnerable.

The precise limits of "Louisiana" were unknown. In the first half of the eighteenth century, French explorers had roamed over a large area west of the Mississippi, and the French had established a major colony near the mouth of the Mississippi, based on New Orleans. Spain claimed Texas, the Southwest, and California, but French Louisiana encompassed a vast area west of the Mississippi River, ranging from the later American state of Louisiana in the south to the Canadian border on the north and westwards to the vicinity of the Rocky Mountains. The area of immediate interest to France in the late 1790s was south of the Red River, including New Orleans, in what was to become the state of Louisiana, but a transfer of territory would include much more than that. In 1800, as Napoleon was taking control of France, the French secured the retrocession of Louisiana from Spain. The secret treaty of San Ildefonso was signed on September 30, within a day of the treaty ending the Quasi-War between France and the United States. The treaty provided for France to receive Louisiana and six warships, and for Spain to receive a kingdom in Italy for the son-in-law of the Spanish monarchs. Napoleon was beginning to readjust the map of Europe. The treaty was secret, for Louisiana would not actually be transferred until the kingdom was recognized by other European powers, and it was also realized that such a transfer would cause great consternation in the United States.

The delay in fulfilling the details of the treaty was longer than expected, and while Napoleon tried to make sure that the kingdom of Etruria in Italy was firmly established, Spain expressed qualms about the future role of the United States in the whole southwest region. To allay these fears, France promised Spain that Louisiana would never be transferred to a third power. Within a year Napoleon was to ignore that promise.

Although the treaty was secret, rumors of its terms quickly spread in Europe and reached the United States in the months after Jefferson assumed office. The rumors were made worse by the assumption that the Floridas as well as Louisiana had been ceded. Jefferson had ample reason to be shocked by the news that Louisiana was again to be French. Napoleon had fallen heir to the gains of the French Revolution and was preparing to drive for what was soon to be imperial glory. It had been bad enough to have an inefficient Spain in command of the lower Mississippi, but a renewed and dynamic France could threaten the United States' position in the whole Mississippi Valley. Since Jay's and Pinckney's treaties in 1794 and 1795, settlers had poured across the Appalachians in great numbers, taking up unsettled lands in Kentucky and Tennessee and moving across the Ohio River in such numbers that Ohio was a state by 1803. American farm produce was flooding down the Mississippi River, and the wharves of New Orleans were crowded with flatboats and barges from all over the Ohio-Mississippi river systems. France would control the commerce of most of the American settlements from the Appalachians to the Mississippi.

Jefferson was also concerned that with powerful France in possession of the territory west of the Mississippi River, his dream of an "empire for liberty" spreading across the whole Mississippi Valley would be threatened. Before he had heard of the Louisiana transfer, Jefferson had already begun to plan an expedition westward through the whole region. The Lewis and Clark expedition of 1803–1806 followed the Missouri River west, crossed the Rockies, and reached the Pacific at the mouth of the Columbia River. Jefferson believed that they were exploring an area that would eventually provide land for America's surplus population. In the immediate future, French possession of Louisiana would threaten the trade and livelihood of America's trans-Appalachian frontiersmen; in the long run, it would threaten the existence of the United States as an agrarian republic. Immediately after Jefferson heard the news that Louisiana was likely to be French, he ordered the rapid acquisition of all possible Indian lands westward to the Mississippi River. Jefferson wanted to get as much territory as he could before the French began to influence the Indians of the region.

In the spring of 1802, Jefferson began his diplomatic strategy to keep the French out of Louisiana. He decided to try to persuade the French that their occupation of the area would drive the United States into the arms of Great Britain. In April 1802, he wrote to Robert R. Livingston, the American minister in France, and sent the letter in the care of Pierre Samuel du Pont de Nemours, a French friend who had been living in the United States. Du Pont was allowed to read the letter. In it Jefferson told Livingston that there was only one spot on the globe "the possessor of which is our natural and habitual enemy"—New Orleans. The produce of three-eighths of United States territory had to pass to market through that spot; soon it would accept more than half of America's produce. "The day that France takes possession of New Orleans," wrote Jefferson, "fixes the sentence which is to restrain her forever within her low-water mark. It seals the union of two nations, who, in conjunction, can maintain exclusive possession of the ocean. From that moment, we must marry ourselves to the British fleet and nation." These were strong words from a man who believed Great Britain to be the main threat to American republicanism, and he intended them more for the French than for Livingston. Du Pont suggested to Jefferson that purchase rather than threats might be the way to proceed. Jefferson, of course, was clearly hoping that he could head off possible conflict by persuading the French that it was not in their interest to proceed with their plans, and, shortly after Jefferson had written to Livingston, Secretary of State James Madison asked Livingston to find out what would be the purchase price for Louisiana and the Floridas. The Americans still assumed that the French were getting the Floridas as well as Louisiana.

Doubts about just what France intended lingered throughout the summer, but sudden action was precipitated by the Spanish, who still occupied the region. In October 1802, following orders from Spain, the Spanish authorities in Louisiana suspended the American right to deposit goods at New Orleans before shipping them via the Gulf of Mexico. This was a Spanish, not a French decision, but it caused an uproar in the United States. Westerners demanded action, because it was generally assumed in the United States that this was the beginning of a new French policy. Spain was to restore the right of deposit in the following year, but by that time Jefferson had taken action in an effort to end the crisis. The Federalists, who had so often been taken to task by Jefferson and Madison for failing to respond to British threats, were now attacking the administration for failing to respond to a French threat. Jefferson had been hoping that when the war in Europe was renewed, and France was cut off from Louisiana by British sea power, he could then achieve a solution, but the suspension of the right of deposit and the outrage in America forced him to take immediate action.

In January 1803 Congress responded to a request from the President and provided $2 million for the use of a mission to France. Du Pont had again written to Jefferson and suggested that the United States could buy New Orleans and the Floridas; he too did not realize that Spain had ceded only Louisiana. Jefferson had decided to send James Monroe to join Livingston in an effort to buy New Orleans and the Floridas. Monroe sailed in March. The instructions he carried authorized the envoys to buy these places for not more than fifty million livres (some $9,375,000), and to guarantee freedom of navigation of the Mississippi River to both countries (Jefferson assumed that France would retain most of the west bank of the Mississippi). If Napoleon would only sell part of what was wanted, the Floridas were to be considered only one-quarter the value of New Orleans and East Florida only half the value of West Florida. To obtain a satisfactory treaty, the envoys were told that they could, if necessary, guarantee to France the possession of all the rest of the Louisiana territory west of the Mississippi River. This demonstrates how disastrously the administration viewed the immediate prospect of the closing of the Mississippi to American trade, for Jefferson, of course, fully expected that American settlers would ultimately settle the area beyond the Mississippi. If France refused to sell and closed the Mississippi, then the envoys were authorized to seek an alliance with Great Britain.

By the time that Monroe arrived in Paris in mid-April the whole situation had undergone a dramatic change, for Napoleon had offered to sell not only New Orleans but also the whole of Louisiana to the United States. He could not offer the Floridas because they were not his to sell. Napoleon's reasons for deciding to sell the whole region were connected both to the situation in the West Indies and in Europe. One of the main reasons why the French wanted Louisiana was to supply provisions to their sugar islands in the West Indies. The most important of these was Santo Domingo, but that island presented major problems to Napoleon. The slaves on the island had tried to apply the original French revolutionary ideals of liberty, equality, and fraternity to their own condition, and in the 1790s had risen in revolt against their French masters. Many plantations were burned and their white owners killed, and refugees fled to the American mainland. Under the leadership of Toussaint L'Ouverture, the blacks on Santo Domingo were successful in resisting the French. Napoleon sent an army to end the revolt, but in 1802, thousands of French soldiers on the island died, most of them of yellow fever. Toussaint L'Ouverture was eventually to be tricked into surrender and died in a French dungeon, but he had succeeded in resisting Napoleon's army. In the fall of 1802, Napoleon prepared to send more men after the others; they could retake Santo Domingo and occupy Louisiana. This second army gathered and prepared to sail, but an early winter kept them in port. In the winter of 1802–1803, Napoleon faced a situation in which the main island that Louisiana was supposed to supply was in disorder.

The situation in Europe was also changing dramatically in the winter of 1802–1803. It was quite obvious that the treaty of Amiens had been a failure and that France and England would soon be at war. This created more problems for Napoleon in the New World. The British commanded the seas. They could prevent the retaking of Santo Domingo, and might even take New Orleans for themselves. Moreover, if the war were renewed in Europe, Napoleon was ready to take to the field. The money that the United States would pay for Louisiana would be extremely useful.

Just before Monroe reached Paris, Talleyrand (who had survived the Directory as he was to survive the fall of Napoleon) asked Livingston what the United States would give for the whole of Louisiana. When Monroe arrived, the two envoys decided to go ahead and buy the whole vast region. Their instructions had authorized them to buy New Orleans and the Floridas for less than $10 million. They finally bought the whole Louisiana territory, including New Orleans, for some $15 million. Not all of this money was to go to France; about $3,750,000 of it was to go to satisfy various claims of American citizens against the French. The agreements were dated April 30, 1803. By the Louisiana purchase, the existing area of the United States had been roughly doubled. Monroe and Livingston had acted alone, for in these years before telegraph or telephone there was no way to communicate with America in time. Napoleon wanted a prompt decision.

Jefferson was delighted, but he had constitutional qualms. He thought that to double the size of the nation and to bring within the union the inhabitants of the new region required a constitutional amendment. The administration was also taken to task by the Federalists, who, reversing their previous emphasis on a broad interpretation of national power, argued that the administration had acted unconstitutionally. This did the Federalists no good, for most Americans realized that the United States had been remarkably fortunate in peacefully obtaining an empire for some $15 million. Jefferson's cabinet persuaded him that, qualms or not, a two-thirds vote in the Senate was easier to obtain than the approval of three-quarters of the states to a constitutional amendment. The Federalists raged, but the Senate approved the treaty. The Louisiana purchase was the high-point of Jefferson's presidency.

Since first hearing of the probable Louisiana cession to France, the American administration had assumed that the

Floridas had also been included in the cession. Spain and France had not dealt for this region, but a flimsy claim could be advanced on the grounds that until 1763 French Louisiana had included not only New Orleans and all the territory west of the Mississippi but also West Florida as far as the Perdido River. East Florida had been Spanish since the sixteenth century. In 1763, New Orleans and French Louisiana west of the Mississippi were transferred from France to Spain, while East and West Florida were taken by Great Britain; the Floridas were given back to Spain by Great Britain in 1783. In 1800 both the French and the Spanish dealt for New Orleans and Louisiana west of the Mississippi, but the wording of the treaty gave no specific boundaries because the western boundaries of French Louisiana had never been defined.

In Paris, after the treaty had been signed, Livingston convinced himself and Monroe that it should be so construed as to include West Florida as far as the Perdido. Jefferson favored this interpretation, and for the rest of his administration he placed great pressure on the Spanish in an effort to obtain at least part of the Floridas. To most Americans it appeared as inevitable and just that the Floridas should be annexed by the United States. The basic interest was commercial and strategic but it also stemmed from a deep belief that it was decreed by providence that the young, virtuous republic should replace old, decadent Spain in control of a vital area of the North American Continent.

At first Jefferson simply proceeded as though West Florida had been included in the Louisiana cession. In February 1804, Congress passed the Mobile Act, which was so worded as to imply that much of West Florida would be included in the revenue district of Mississippi. The Spanish, who had protested Napoleon's cession of Louisiana to the United States as a violation of their agreement with France, objected vigorously to the Mobile Act. From this time until he retired from the presidency, Jefferson made determined efforts to get at least part of the Floridas for the United States. In the spring of 1804, James Monroe was instructed to proceed to Madrid to join the American minister, Charles Pinckney, in an effort to obtain the

Floridas. It was hoped that this question could be linked with an American demand for the Spanish payment of various spoliation claims. The negotiations were a failure. Spain had no desire to yield part of the Floridas to the United States.

When Jefferson heard of the failure of Monroe's mission he again talked, as at the time of the Louisiana crisis, of the possibility of an alliance with England. Jefferson was worried that France was ready to take Spain's part in its quarrel with the United States. A possible way out of the impasse seemed to present itself when Talleyrand let it be known that the Floridas might be available for money. Napoleon hoped to siphon off any purchase price from Spain in the form of subsidies to France. Late in 1805, Jefferson decided that while publicly talking in a threatening manner he would send a secret message to Congress to request money to buy the Floridas. The proposal ran into a hornet's nest in Congress, and was not passed until February 1806. When Virginian John Randolph, who had been a close ally of Jefferson's, realized that the plan was an indirect way of bribing France to get the Floridas from Spain, he broke with the administration. This ensured that the government would now be lashed with piercing invective, for the brilliant, eccentric Randolph, with his cutting, almost soprano voice, delighted in lambasting the inconsistencies of his foes. Jefferson's plan was all to no avail, for by the time the proposal was ready to be presented in Europe, Napoleon had changed his mind. Jefferson consistently believed that corrupt Spain had no right to hold a colony in an area vital to the young republic, but he was obliged to leave office without obtaining the Floridas.

The failure to obtain at least part of the Floridas irritated Jefferson, but it was not the question of the Floridas but the renewal of the war in Europe that eventually created difficulties for the Republicans that exceeded those faced by the Federalists in the years after 1793. The rupture of the peace of Amiens in the spring of 1803 led to wars that were more intense and far-reaching than those of the 1790s. The most important difference was that Napoleon's ambitions and success placed greater pressure on the British than they had experienced before 1801.

Immediately following the renewal of war in 1803, Napoleon made preparations to invade England; when that endeavor proved impossible, he hoped to defeat England by conquering much of Europe, overcoming England's continental allies, and excluding British trade from the continent. On their part, the British, to an extent previously unknown, felt that their very existence depended on sea power. Only the British navy seemed capable of stopping Napoleon's triumphant progress. In this situation, there was not the slightest hope of untroubled neutral trade. There were great neutral profits to be made from trading to Europe in time of all-out war, but there were also great dangers to be faced, dangers that would necessitate an official governmental response.

The years from 1803 to 1807 were extremely profitable ones for American commerce. The European demand for American agricultural produce was high, but the most dramatic growth was in the carrying trade in the goods of other nations. From 1805 to 1807, the trade in re-exports from the United States was greater than that in domestic produce; much of this re-export trade was in the products of the West Indies. Although the British had declared a blockade of parts of the European coast in 1804, American ships were hardly hindered from their lucrative trade from the French West Indies to Europe. Even less hindered was the very heavy American trade with Great Britain, for the French navy was usually in port until defeated by Nelson at Trafalgar in October 1805. The French had to depend heavily on their privateers if they wished to harass neutral trade with Great Britain.

The most pressing problem faced by the Americans in the months immediately following the renewal of the war in Europe was a great increase in the British practice of impressment. From 1803 to 1805 the British feared that they were about to be invaded. Napoleon massed his troops and invasion vessels in the Channel ports, and England desperately needed sailors to man her ships. Between 1803 and 1806, more seamen were impressed from American vessels than in the whole period from 1793 to 1801. British seamen continued to flee harsh conditions on their own ships and served on American vessels. British ships stopped American merchantmen looking for British seamen and frequently took Americans either by accident or design. In a time of national danger, British sea captains were not cautious about stopping neutral vessels, nor were they cautious about just who they impressed to fill out their crews. As a result, several thousand Americans were impressed into the British service in the years before the War of 1812. The shipowners of New England often regarded impressment as simply another hazard of foreign trade in a time of general war, but it was an issue that could stir indignation in Americans in areas far removed from the coast. To Republicans it was yet another example of the manner in which Great Britain flouted the rights of the United States.

Particularly infuriating to patriotic Americans was the manner in which the British hovered off the American coast in the vicinity of the major ports, stopping and searching ships and removing seamen. This was a constant problem in the years after the renewal of war, and early in 1804 a bill was introduced in Congress that would have empowered the President to prohibit the supplying of ships that had impressed seamen from American ships. The bill was not strongly supported, for American opinion was still pleased both by the vast trade opportunities and by the comparative moderation of British blockading policies. In September 1804, Jefferson wrote that "the new administration in England is entirely cordial. There has never been a time when our flag was so little molested by them in the European seas, or irregularities there so readily & respectfully corrected."

In 1804 and 1805, Jefferson's major interest in foreign policy was still his effort to obtain part of the Floridas from Spain. From December 1804, Spain was at war with England, and Jefferson was hopeful that this might lead to a situation in which it would be simple for the United States to obtain Florida. He was also temporarily pushed toward England because Spain was now an ally of France. Most of Jefferson's optimism about the results of the French Revolution had now disappeared. He held no illusions about Napoleon. In 1805, he was concerned that France would throw her weight behind Spain in America and that this would necessitate closer American ties with Great Britain. As late as August 1805, Jefferson suggested to members of his cabinet that it might be necessary to secure an alliance with England if there were hostile conduct on the part of Spain or France.

CRISIS WITH ENGLAND

Any hope that Jefferson might have that Great Britain intended to pursue a friendly course toward American neutral commerce disappeared rapidly in the last years of his second administration. The root of Jefferson's and America's problems was that in the years following 1803, many in England were demanding stricter policies against neutral trade with France and her possessions. These demands came both from patriots who argued that American commerce was bolstering the power of Napoleon and from British shipping and West India interests who feared that the United States shipping interests were using the opportunities provided by the war to expand into major competition with the British. Opponents of a generous policy toward neutral trade stressed that any expansion of the American merchant marine at the expense of British shipping would reduce England's overall power, for the merchant marine was the nursery of British seamen, and on the British navy depended England's ascendency in world affairs.

The British response to the internal pressures and to the growth of American trade with France and her possessions began to take a decisive form in July 1805. In that month, a British appeals court declared in the *Essex* decision that the "broken voyage" as it was being practiced by the Americans was illegal. American shippers who carried goods to an American port to break their journey between the French West India colonies and France would have to show a genuine intention to import the goods into the United States by the payment of regular import duties; otherwise the voyage would be regarded as continuous and the ships and goods liable to seizure by British vessels. As in 1793, the British failed to give fair warning to the Americans that a new policy was to be implemented, and in the summer and fall of 1805 a great many seizures were made in the Caribbean.

For many in England the *Essex* decision was not enough, and considerable pressure was exerted for a more stringent policy. In October 1805, in his pamphlet *War in Disguise,* James Stephen argued that the United States had taken advantage of the European war to build an extensive commerce between the French West Indies and France. This, he argued, had enhanced Napoleon's power to wage war against Great Britain and had increased the maritime strength of the United States to the point where it was presenting a threat to British maritime supremacy. Stephen argued that the American carrying trade between the French colonies and France should be ended.

England's ability to control American commerce was being enhanced in the very month that Stephen's pamphlet was published. At the battle of Trafalgar the British fleet inflicted a total defeat on the combined French and Spanish fleets. England now ruled the waves as never before. But while Great Britain completed control of the ocean, Napoleon was fast achieving domination on the continent of Europe. Less than two months after Trafalgar, he defeated the Austrian and Russian armies at the battle of Austerlitz. Late in the following year he was to win crushing victories over the Prussians. The seas around Europe were under British control, but the land mass of Europe, from the Channel to the borders of Russia, was falling under the control of France.

Since assuming power in 1801, the Republicans had been fortunate in the degree to which American trade had been allowed to flourish in what since 1803 had been a period of escalating European conflict. The Federalist concessions to Great Britain, and Adams's achievement of peace with France in 1800, had laid a sound basis for an expanding American carrying trade with a minimum interference from the belligerents.

This happy situation was now coming to an end. The *Essex* decision was only the beginning. With one European belligerent supreme on the land, and the other on the sea, blockade and counterblockade were to become a vital method of inflicting far-reaching damage on the enemy. When to this was added the jealousy of British shipping and West India interests at American commercial expansion, it was clear that American commerce was entering a difficult and dangerous period.

Jefferson's optimism about Anglo-American relations, which had persisted through the summer of 1805, began to lessen in the following winter as news of British seizures poured into American ports. There was little doubt about the direction in which Jefferson and his Secretary of State Madison would lead the United States in response to the new British infringements of American neutral rights. Jefferson hated war and militarism, and since 1801 had reduced the American military forces. He had great faith, however, in the economic worth of United States trade with the European powers, and believed that the United States could show the traditional powers of Europe that force was not the only answer to the failure of diplomacy. After becoming President he had suggested to Robert Livingston, the American minister to France, that neutral rights could not be best enforced by war: "Those peaceable coercions which are in the power of every nation, if undertaken in concert & in time of peace, are more likely to produce the desired effect." In the 1790s, James Madison had advocated commercial discrimination against England, and like Jefferson he believed that commercial pressures could be used to change the policies of the European powers.

In response to the new flurry of British seizures and the continuation of impressment, Madison in January 1806, reported to Congress Britain's infringements of American neutral rights. Also, in the same month, Congressmen were able to read Madison's new pamphlet, *An Examination of the British Doctrine,* which at great length disputed the legality of the British Rule of 1756, by which a trade closed in time of peace could not be opened in time of war. Congress discussed the new wave of British seizures and, in response both to these and the nagging problem of impressment, in April 1806, passed a Non-Importation Act which prohibited the importation from Great Britain of a long list of articles—including flax, hemp, tin, and brass—which could be produced in the United States or imported from other countries. The act was to go into effect in November if no settlement was arranged, but, in the hope of reaching agreement, Jefferson delayed the measure until the end of 1807.

Jefferson was placing his hopes for settlement on a new special mission to England. Such a mission had been urged on Jefferson by American merchants who were hoping that something in the manner of Jay's Treaty could be achieved; they were to find, however, that the British were now less inclined to treat American commerce leniently, and that while the Republicans were prepared to negotiate they were not ready to concede as much as the Federalists to the British position.

American hopes of a settlement were increased because of a change in the British government. The death of William Pitt in January 1806 had brought into power a Whig ministry that was friendlier to the United States than the Tory government which had preceded it. This change renewed Jefferson's optimism about Anglo-American relations. He thought that it ensured the United States a "just settlement." In March, Jefferson decided to send William Pinkney of Maryland to join James Monroe, the American minister in England. They were to negotiate a treaty that would include a British abandonment of the right of impressment and a return to the "broken voyage" system; and they were also to replace those commercial sections of Jay's Treaty that were about to expire.

The American envoys had no chance whatever of achieving what Jefferson wanted. Although the Whig ministry that ruled Great Britain from the death of Pitt to March 1807 was less hostile toward the United States than the Tory government that was to replace it, it had to respond in England to those who argued that the American carrying trade was allowing the French to circumvent the British blockade. The Whigs were also obliged to listen to the British Admiralty, and the Admiralty insisted that the right of impressment was essential to the maintenance of British naval power. The Whig ministry, however, influenced by British merchants who defended the importance of the American trade to Great Britain, did not attempt to destroy the American carrying trade in the manner advocated by the British shipping and West India interests. Although "Fox's blockade" of May 1806 declared a paper blockade of a vast stretch of the European coast from the Elbe River to Brest, it was to be enforced strictly only from the Seine to Ostend. Outside that area neutrals could trade if they were not coming from an enemy port. Fox's blockade was disliked and objected to by the United States, but it was also viewed as too moderate a policy by those in England who wished to crush the neutral carrying trade between the French colonies and France.

Monroe and Pinkney experienced in London a situation very like that experienced by John Jay in 1794. To obtain a treaty, they had to waive any major British concessions on impressment or neutral rights. The British would not give up the right of impressment. The subject was omitted from the treaty, and the British merely submitted a note to the American commissioners promising that care would be taken not to impress American citizens. The British were somewhat more yielding on the question of American trade between the French colonies and France. Goods could be taken from the French West Indies colonies to unblockaded ports in France and Spain, provided that a 2 percent duty was paid in the United States; and goods could be taken from those countries to the colonies provided a 1 percent duty was paid in the United States.

The long negotiations ended in the signing of the treaty in December 1806. The United States had obtained very little, but it was the best possible treaty in the circumstances. Many in England were clamoring for more stringent policies against the United States. If the United States wished to continue its lucrative trade to Europe, it would have to continue on British sufferance or not at all. Great Britain had the naval power to place severe restrictions on American trade, to stop and search American merchant ships, and to impress those believed to be British deserters. Most American shippers were happy enough with the profits that they would put up with the harassment. Jefferson and many of his Republican supporters were not. They wished to assert America's right to trade in time of war, and they believed that American trade was so necessary to Europe that the policies of the European powers could be changed by commercial restrictions and discrimination. Unlike Hamilton and the Federalists, they believed the trade of the United States was more important to Great Britain than the trade of Great Britain was to the United States. To achieve their ends, they were prepared to take actions which would severely damage the economy of the United States.

Jefferson would not submit the Monroe-Pinkney treaty to the Senate for ratification. His primary objection was the British refusal to make treaty concessions regarding impressment. He wanted to continue negotiations, but if commercial warfare against England was called for, then he would have commercial warfare. In the winter of 1806–1807, while waiting for the treaty from England, Jefferson was thinking of non-importation as a viable alternative to persuade Great Britain to change her policies. He was soon obliged to think of stronger measures, for the restrictions on American trade and British maritime aggression increased dramatically from November 1806 to November 1807.

The first blow in the new and far more intense round of European commercial warfare was delivered by Napoleon in November 1806 in his Berlin Decree. This decree declared the British islands in a state of blockade and prohibited all trade in British merchandise. French ports were closed to vessels coming directly from England or her colonies. Napoleon did not have the naval strength to blockade England, but as his armies advanced across Europe and as more and more continental nations came under his control, he wished to bring about England's commercial ruin by preventing the sale of her goods in Europe. Napoleon's Continental System would be his answer to British blockades.

In 1807, Great Britain responded to Napoleon and also

took steps to satisfy those who wished to stop the American merchant marine from aiding Napoleon and growing at the expense of England. The British Order in Council issued in January was comparatively moderate. This order prohibited vessels from trading between ports in the hands of France or French allies. In March, however, the English Whig government fell, and the new Tory ministry rapidly formulated plans to control all neutrals trading with France. In November 1807, Orders in Council were issued which declared a complete blockade of France and all enemy countries. Trade with these areas was prohibited except under British license. Now American trade would be subject to specific British regulations. American ships could still trade with France and French possessions but only after coming to a British port and obtaining a British license. Britain wished to control all trade with France, not only to stop supplies reaching Napoleon, but also to ensure that any trade which did take place would swell the flow of bullion into England.

In the spring of 1807, Jefferson and Madison were chiefly concerned with the possibility of re-opening the Monroe-Pinkney negotiations, but any hopes they had of continuing these discussions were shattered by the events of the spring and early summer. In March, news arrived of the January Order in Council, in April, of the formation of a Tory government, and in June, of bloodshed off the American coast. This last caused a major crisis. Since 1804, British warships had been hovering off the American coast, stopping and searching American merchant ships, and removing suspected British deserters. This stirred American popular indignation and also led to incidents. In April 1806, an American merchant seaman was killed off New York when a British ship fired into the American merchant vessel it was trying to stop. This incident caused a near-riot in New York city, but it was played down by the government which still had high hopes that the Monroe-Pinkney mission would arrange a settlement.

In June 1807, a far more serious incident occurred at a time when Anglo-American relations were already rapidly deteriorating. A number of seamen had deserted from British warships lying off Chesapeake Bay, had gone into Norfolk, Virginia, taunted the British officers who had tried to arrange for their return, and had enlisted on American ships. The British suspected that some had enlisted on the American frigate *Chesapeake*. On hearing of this, the British naval commander-in-chief at Halifax, Nova Scotia, Vice-Admiral George Berkeley, ordered that the *Chesapeake* should be stopped and searched if it put to sea. This decision was made on his own authority. The British government had never claimed the right to impress seamen from warships of another power for that was a direct violation of national sovereignty.

On June 22, the *Chesapeake* put to sea. Near the American coast, the British frigate *Leopard* signalled the *Chesapeake* to heave to, sent a boarding party, and asked for the handing over of deserters. The captain of the *Chesapeake* refused, but when he attempted to get underway the British fired into his ship. Three American seamen were killed and eighteen wounded. The *Chesapeake* struck its colors, and the British went on board and took off four seamen. One was subsequently proved to be a British deserter, and he was hanged. The other three, two of them blacks, were subsequently proved to be Americans. One died in British captivity, the other two were eventually returned to the United States.

The *Chesapeake* affair was a far greater insult and injury than the Federalists had endured from either the British or the French, although it could well be argued that this incident was the result not of the definite intent of the British government but rather of the irresponsible actions of a subordinate. The American reaction was intense. Popular meetings were held all over the country to denounce the British and to demand governmental action. At no time in the entire period of the Revolutionary and Napoleonic wars was American opinion so unified as in the immediate aftermath of the *Chesapeake* affair.

Jefferson's initial reaction was to avoid war. Although he ordered British armed ships to leave American waters, he made it clear that he believed that only Congress could decide the question of peace or war. Congress was not called into session until the fall, and in the meantime the American government demanded that the British disavow the action of the *Leopard* and return the four seamen. Moreover, Jefferson insisted that the British should promise to end the practice of impressment from American ships. This ensured that the *Chesapeake* affair would drag on for years, for though the British realized they had been in the wrong in the specific case of the *Chesapeake,* they would not tie the solution of this case to the general question of impressment.

Jefferson's role was crucial in 1807. He could have had war in the weeks immediately following the attack on the *Chesapeake*. In his detailed monograph on the Embargo, Bernard Spivak has argued that Jefferson actually wanted war in 1807, but Jefferson's actions and words more suggest a man who feared war might come but still hoped to avoid it. If Jefferson had taken a strong line, immediately brought Congress into special session, and asked for war against England, he would have received strong public backing. But Jefferson was cautious. At heart he wanted war with neither England nor France, although he was not prepared to go as far as Hamilton and Washington to seek British friendship and maintain trade connections. Jefferson wanted markets for American produce, and he was also coming to realize that he had an obligation to defend the American carrying trade, but he was still hopeful that the United States could achieve her ends through peaceful means.

As the summer passed, Jefferson's optimism diminished. The British were in no mood to compromise and had not the slightest intention of settling the *Chesapeake* affair if it would mean agreeing to end impressment from American ships. They were preparing for harsher, not softer measures against neutrals. Rather than abandoning impressment, England in October issued an order recalling all her seamen from foreign service and instructed British officers to seize these men from foreign merchant ships. News of this latest evidence of British intransigence reached Washington in mid-December at the same time as the news that Napoleon was seizing American ships under the provisions of his Berlin Decree of the previous year. There were also strong rumors in newspapers and private letters that England was preparing a major blow against neutral commerce. Thus Jefferson, even before he had formal notice of the comprehensive British Orders in Council of November 1807, knew that England was taking a hard line.

ECONOMIC COERCION

In the late summer and early fall, Jefferson came to believe that war with England was likely and even necessary, but he had no real belief in war as a solution to America's problems. His caution in the early summer had cooled public opinion, and even in the late fall, when he thought that war might be the only solution for British intransigence, he exercised no decisive, bellicose leadership. Reluctant to take a firm step toward war, Congress first enforced against Great Britain the Non-Importation Act against selected British products that had been passed in the previous year, and then, on December 22, accepted Jefferson's recommendation for an embargo on the departure of American vessels for foreign ports. Foreign ships could leave in ballast or with the goods they had on board when notified of the Embargo Act. Imports in foreign vessels were still permitted, except for those items from Great Britain that were banned under the provisions of the Non-Importation Act, but such trade was severely hindered because these ships could not take American produce out of the country.

As Jefferson had drifted from believing that he could secure a peaceful redress of grievances to the feeling that war might well be necessary, the embargo had dual advantages. It would remove American ships from possible attack, while at the same time exerting pressure on Great Britain to change her maritime policies. Once in place, the embargo quickly was to become a broad attempt at economic coercion rather than a temporary measure designed to leave the United States with options. Jefferson, along with Madison and many other Republicans, had long believed that in its trade the United States held the power to change the policies of the European powers, particularly Great Britain, through peaceful means. When, in 1808, Jefferson persisted in the embargo as a measure of economic coercion, it far better suited his own instincts and beliefs than a resort to war. Jefferson was prone at times of crisis with the main European powers to talk or write of the likelihood of war, but he always ended by seeking peace rather than war as a means of achieving American desires.

Jefferson now hoped that while British factories cried out for American cotton, British manufacturers and exporters would press the British government to open the American market that had been partly closed to them. Jefferson was right in these expectations, but wrong in his belief that this would force a major change in British policies. The Tory government was less beholden to the manufacturers and the American merchants than to the shipping and the West India interests. The latter were delighted that the United States was withholding her shipping from the oceans of the world. Also, the impact of American economic coercion was minimized by the opening of South American trade to the British at this time. Late in 1807, the trade of Brazil became available when the Portuguese royal family fled there to escape a French invasion, and in 1808, the rest of Latin America was opened up when the Spanish rose in revolt against French troops and sided with the British. Yet, commercial factors aside, the British would not yield to Jefferson's embargo, for they believed that victory over Napoleon and their greatness as a nation depended upon vigorous assertion of their maritime rights.

The tragedy of the Embargo Act was that it effectively ruined American commerce without producing the desired effects in Europe. Great Britain continued to shape maritime policies to suit its war aims and the desires of commercial interests, not the wishes of the United States. Moreover, French policies toward neutrals were as ruthless as those of the British, and became particularly burdensome even while the Embargo was being enforced in the United States. In December 1807, less than a week before the United States enacted the embargo, Napoleon issued the Milan Decree in response to the November British Orders in Council. The Milan Decree declared that every ship that had submitted to British search, travelled to England, or paid an English tax was considered to have become English property, and all such ships were liable to seizure either at sea or on entering French ports. In addition, England was declared in a state of blockade, and any ship sailing to or from Great Britain or her possessions was liable to seizure.

After the British Orders in Council and the French decrees, neutrals, in theory, were in danger of seizure wherever they sailed in Europe. If they did not go to Great Britain to be licensed, they could be seized by the British; if they did go, they could be seized by the French. In spite of all this, neutrals could still make a great profit from European trade. These comprehensive blockades were paper blockades. There was no way the British could effectively close the coasts they declared blockaded. Also, good profits could still be made by trading under British license, and a British license would not necessarily mean seizure by the French, for the French needed certain British manufactured goods. Many neutral ships would be seized and seamen impressed, but for those who were prepared to take the risks there were great profits to be made from countries starved for goods and shipping.

Many American ships participated in European trade even during the embargo. Ships that were still abroad often stayed abroad and engaged in the carrying trade. Other ships broke the Embargo Act regulations when they left American ports. There was also extensive smuggling between the United States and Canada. Evasions became more difficult during 1808 and early 1809, for Congress enacted a series of measures designed to uphold the law. The Federalist shipowners of New England hated the embargo with a passion, and they accused Jefferson of maliciously destroying their trade. By late 1808, the United States was badly divided and economically much worse off than she had been in 1807. An irony of the embargo as a coercive measure was that when it failed it left the United States much less united and much weaker than before it began. This placed the government in the invidious position of either removing the embargo and admitting failure, or declaring war when too weak and disunited to be effective.

While the United States suffered and seethed, the British government was complacent. Viscount Castlereagh, the British Secretary for War and the Colonies, stated in the spring of 1808 that "I look upon the embargo as operating at present more forcibly in our favor than any measure of hostility we could call forth were war actually declared." And, in spite of the extreme tensions between the United States and Great Britain, Napoleon, now dominating Europe, was in no mood to curry the favor of the United States. In April 1808, he decided to take advantage of the fact that many American ships were still trading in Europe despite the American embargo. In that month, he issued the Bayonne Decree which confiscated all American ships in French ports on the grounds that as the United States had declared an embargo these must be British ships in disguise.

In 1807 and 1808 the Republicans discovered that the United States carried no weight in Europe. Since 1776 many Americans had overestimated the persuasive power of United States commerce, which the Republicans had made a cornerstone of their foreign policy. When the Federalists had been confronted by British maritime aggression, they had largely acquiesced in the British interpretation of neutral rights, but Jefferson and the Republicans had turned to measures of economic retaliation, which they had long advocated as a means of achieving the commercial ends of the United States. The decision to use some form of economic retaliation had merit. It avoided war, calmed down the patriots who asked for some action against British aggression, and brought pressure to bear on England that might eventually lead to modest concessions. The Republican mistake was in leading off with a draconian embargo; a measure that hurt the United States more than it hurt Great Britain. It shattered American trade and finances, created bitter internal opposition, and left no possibility of stepping up the pressure on Great Britain by further escalation of the economic measures.

The last months of Jefferson's presidency were sad ones.

Jefferson longed for retirement and Monticello, and the Congress that met in November 1808 was uncertain as to how it should proceed. The embargo had to go, but what should replace it was not readily apparent. The country was weak militarily and ill-prepared for war, and the Federalist opposition thought that war with Great Britain would be madness. Although the United States had cause for declaring war on both the greatest sea power and the greatest land power in the world, it did not require great wisdom to perceive that this would be unwise. For a time the United States was to submerge feelings of injured pride in an attempt to end the rabid internal dissention, to find a market for America's farmers, and commerce for America's shippers. For while the Federalists had screamed that Jefferson was destroying the shipping interests of New England, he was actually levelling a still heavier blow against the plantation owners and farmers of his own party who had grown to depend on foreign markets and who had not the financial resources of those who had grown rich on the profits of the wartime carrying trade.

The simple anger against England of the summer of 1807 had become far more complicated by the early months of 1809. Many of the Federalists were now much angrier at Jefferson than at England, for his embargo had done more to ruin their trade than England had done by its commercial regulations. Also, there was now considerable animosity against the French as a result of the variety of seizures and the infamous Bayonne Decree. Congress wanted to express its resentment against both powers but was more anxious to renew some American foreign trade than it was to commit the country to the dangers of war. The solution was an uneasy compromise which left many feeling that the honor of the country had been besmirched. On March 1, 1809, just before he left office, Jefferson signed an act repealing the embargo. It was replaced by the Non-Intercourse Act, which prohibited trade with France or England. Indirect trade with those countries would, however, now be possible through other countries, and many American ship captains were prepared to sail illegally to British ports. The embargo had failed.

When the new President, James Madison, took office in March 1809, he had to govern a country much different from that which Jefferson had begun to govern in 1801. American trade had been shattered by the embargo, and not until after the War of 1812 was it again to reach the heights of the years before 1808. The Federalists were convinced that the Republicans had been duped by France, and the Federalists still believed that the United States should seek friendship with Great Britain. Among the Republicans there was confusion and a sense of failure, and some were beginning to think that war was preferable to the present degradation, even though the military forces were still pitifully weak and the prohibition of British imports by the Non-Intercourse Act gave a further blow to American governmental revenues.

Madison's strengths were ill-designed for America's situation in 1809. As a man of quiet intellectual depth and great integrity, he had been at his best in the shaping of the constitution in 1787. But unlike Jefferson he was unable to inspire confidence in those around him. He was short in stature, slightly built, and soft of voice. Henry Clay was later to say of him that he was "wholly unfit for the storms of War. Nature has cast him in too benevolent a mould." This was a harsh judgment, but it was generally agreed that Madison was not a dynamic leader.

The process by which the United States eventually decided that war was the only alternative to the present dilemma was begun by the failure of the embargo. It was given an additional impetus by the bitter disappointments of the spring and summer of 1809. In April, the British minister to the United States, David Erskine, a friend of America who had been appointed by the brief-lived Whig ministry, misinterpreted his instructions from London and signed an agreement by which Great Britain agreed to remove the Orders in Council in return for the United States removing the Non-Intercourse Act against Great Britain. The news was greeted in the United States with universal joy, and hundreds of ships left for British ports. A number of ominous signs from England tempered American optimism before, late in July, there came the shocking news that Great Britain had repudiated the Erskine agreement. This confirmed all that the Republicans had long believed about the perfidy of England and its hatred for the United States.

In April 1809, Great Britain had altered its commercial policies in Europe but not in a manner to appease the United States. In that month, a new Order in Council opened part of French-controlled Europe to neutral trade. The British ministry had decided that a general blockade of Europe, with trade allowed under British license, would be replaced by a more stringent blockade over a more limited area. The new blockade was to extend from the Ems in northern Germany down to Pesaro and Orbitello in Italy; trade with Holland, France, and Napoleon's kingdom of Italy was now to be banned completely. Even outside that area it was specifically stated that there was to be no American trade involving the French colonies. American shipping could now engage in trade to certain parts of Europe, but Great Britain intended to enforce a complete prohibition on American trade between the French colonies and Europe.

The United States was often irritated by Napoleon's sporadic forays against American commerce, but this irritation did not equal the despair and disgust felt by the Republicans at the manner in which Great Britain calmly issued elaborate regulations governing most of America's foreign trade. It was as though the United States was losing its status as an independent republic and sinking back into colonial status. Many Americans were also appalled by the British government's unwillingness to grant any concessions in direct negotiation. Erskine was recalled after the fiasco of his agreement. He was replaced by Francis James Jackson, a man notorious for his hard-line British attitudes, and his instructions were so rigid that, within two months of his arrival in Washington in September 1809, the United States government broke off negotiations. The British government was obliged to recall him in April 1810, but not before Jackson had further infuriated the American government by communicating with the Federalists and encouraging those who disagreed with Republican policies. In January 1810, Madison suggested in a private letter that the European belligerents might well decide America's policy by leaving no choice "between absolute disgrace and resistance by force." A remaining dilemma was deciding just who to fight, because Napoleon continued to lacerate American feelings and harass American commerce. In March 1810, he repeated his device of the earlier Bayonne Decree when, in the Rambouillet Decree, he announced the seizure of all American ships in French ports on the grounds that as there was an American non-intercourse act in force they must all be British ships in disguise.

The opportunity to distinguish between the hostility and harassment of the British and the French came as a result of a desperate measure passed by Congress in May 1810. The unnerved Eleventh Congress had been unable to agree on how to deal with the continued maritime insults and injuries. In desperation it enacted Macon's Bill No. 2. This measure opened commerce with everyone, including Great Britain and France, but stated that should either Britain or France remove their edicts against American commerce by March 3, 1811, non-intercourse would be again enforced against the other power if it did not also remove its restrictions.

Napoleon quickly saw the opportunity presented by Macon's Bill No. 2. England controlled the seas, but if Napoleon said he would comply with the terms of the new act, then the United States would cut off trade with England while continuing it with France. In August 1810, the French Foreign Minister, the Duc de Cadore, informed the American minister to France that the French decrees against American commerce could be considered revoked as of November 1, 1810. In reality, Napoleon did not end his sporadic seizures of American ships, but it was to take many months for the American government to realize that fact. By that time, the United States had taken decisive steps against Great Britain. At the beginning of November 1810, Madison announced that unless Great Britain removed her Orders in Council against American shipping by February 1, non-intercourse would be renewed against that country. Great Britain refused to act, and beginning in February 1811 non-intercourse operated against Great Britain but not against France.

Although it could be said that Madison had been duped by Napoleon, there had never been any doubt that the Republicans considered Great Britain to be the main enemy. Since 1790 Madison had been interested in breaking the United States' commercial dependence on Great Britain, and Britain's actions in the wars since 1793 had served to convince the Republicans that in war as well as in peace Great Britain was determined to control and throttle the commerce of the infant republic. To many Americans, Great Britain had always presented a serious threat to the stability, prosperity, and even continued existence of the new republic. If, after 1805, Napoleon had wooed rather than chastised the Americans, he could probably have had the United States as a friendly neutral, and embroiled her with Great Britain at a much earlier date. The Republicans no longer admired France, but they knew full well that Great Britain, not France, was their most significant enemy, because Great Britain had the power to inflict more damage. Not only did it control the seas, it also owned Canada, and in the years immediately preceding the War of 1812 this again was becoming a factor of significance in Anglo-American relations.

In the aftermath of Jay's Treaty and Anthony Wayne's victory over the Indians in 1794, the United States appeared to have achieved the stability and security along its northern borders that it had sought since the beginning of the Revolution. In the following years tens of thousands of American settlers poured across the Ohio River, and for more than ten years after Jay's Treaty, the British pursued a peaceful policy in the Old Northwest. After withdrawing from Detroit and Mackinac they established new posts on the Canadian side of the border at St. Joseph's and Amherstburg, but they did not pursue an active policy among the Indians within American territory. Indians from the American side of the border still visited the British posts, but the British reduced the amount of supplies given to them and did not try to enlist them in a border struggle against the Americans.

The situation in the Old Northwest underwent a dramatic change in the aftermath of the crisis produced by the *Chesapeake* affair in the early summer of 1807. As in 1793, the British authorities in Canada decided that war was likely, that in the event of war the United States would invade Canada, and that in such case the cooperation of the Indians would be vital for British resistance. In the last months of 1807, British Indian agents at Amherstburg, on the Canadian side of the border near Detroit, were again ordered to pursue actively the friendship of the Indian tribes within American territory. The object was to enlist the support of these tribes for any future war between Great Britain and the United States. To secure this support, the agents again increased the issuing of supplies to the Indians and also reminded the Indians of the manner in which the Americans were stealing their lands and destroying their way of life.

The British had little difficulty in enlisting Indian support, for the rush of settlers across the Ohio River and Jefferson's keen desire for land westward to the Mississippi had produced a new rash of land cessions in the years after 1802. Tribes which had believed, as the United States told them, that the line drawn at Greenville in 1795 was a permanent line, were now sadly disillusioned. The governor of Indiana Territory, William Henry Harrison, followed Jefferson's orders and pressured the Indian tribes of the region into ceding a vast area throughout the Old Northwest. By 1805, this new pressure had produced a major Indian resistance movement led by the Shawnee Prophet (Tenskwatawa) and his brother, Tecumseh. The Prophet preached a nativistic revival, in which the Indians were urged to throw off white ways and return to the ways of their ancestors. Tecumseh eventually used his brother's religious movement as the basis for a political movement in which he urged the tribes of the Mississippi Valley to unite and oppose any further land cessions. From 1807, the British Indian agents took advantage of the Indian resistance movement in their efforts to win allies for any future war with the United States. Tecumseh was courted by British agents at Amherstburg, and he was encouraged in his efforts to resist further land cessions.

From 1807, Governor Harrison and other American officials continually warned the government in Washington that dangerous Indian resistance was developing in the Old Northwest, and they blamed the British for inspiring it. Harrison's letters to Washington were filled with tales of British intrigue among the Indians within American territory. Such accounts revived the old fears that American security was deeply threatened by the British presence in Canada, and they also had a particularly strong effect on representatives from the recently settled states of Kentucky, Tennessee, and Ohio.

These new states of the Mississippi Valley had been constantly reminded of British power in the preceding years, for the region had been profoundly disturbed by the widespread disruption of American exports brought about by British blockades and American economic retaliation. The new trans-Appalachian settlers of the United States were fervently Republican and fervently patriotic. In the years since the Revolution, they had torn lands away from the Indians in bloody conflict, had built prosperous farms, and were now sending produce down the Mississippi River to New Orleans and the sea. They had long hated any British or Spanish agents who gave aid and comfort to the Indians, they had talked of war when it seemed as though France had been about to close off the Mississippi in 1802, and by 1810 they were bitter at the British for the commercial regulations that played havoc with their export of farm produce. For the Embargo Act and the Non-Intercourse Act they blamed the British government, not Jefferson and Madison. Since 1807 the Mississippi Valley had been suffering economic depression. Prices for farm produce were down while prices for imports were up. The depression stemmed from marketing problems in the valley as well as from maritime conflict, but the British were blamed for the whole situation. In a similar manner the far more numerous Republican representatives from the South Atlantic plantation states were willing to support the economic coercion policies of Jefferson and Madison while blaming the British for their depressed economic state.

It was a young eager politician from beyond the mountains who first caught the imagination of the country in calling for more extreme action against Great Britain. In February 1810, Henry Clay of Kentucky told the Senate, where he was serving out the unexpired term of a previous member, that peaceful resistance had failed, and the time had come for "resistance by the *sword.*" He acknowledged that there were good reasons for war against either England or France, but he maintained that England was the worst offender. British slavery on the seas could be revenged because Canada was vulnerable: "The conquest of Canada is in your power." By taking Canada, the United States in one stroke could have revenge for a whole list of maritime injuries while providing for American security.

Clay's fervor was not enough to inspire the enervated Eleventh Congress. They went home after passing Macon's Bill No. 2. But, in the fall of 1810, elections were held for a new Congress, a Congress that would not assemble until the fall of 1811. In solidly Republican areas in the West and the South, and even in some of the Republican regions adjacent to the last Federalist strongholds in the Northeast, the voters elected to the new House of Representatives a group of generally younger men who were willing to support Clay's cry for stronger action. These were young men who had not fought in the Revolution, and who felt that the glorious history of those years had been tarnished by years of submission to the old enemy, Great Britain. If the victories of the Revolution were to be preserved, if the Republic was to survive and prosper, then its rights would have to be asserted.

The new spirit was muted until the fall of 1811, for in the winter of 1810–1811 it was the old Eleventh Congress that assembled to decide on a course of action. To a large degree, what they had to do followed logically from Madison's proclamation of the previous November. In the early months of 1811 Congress debated enforcing non-intercourse against Great Britain. Although some pointed out that there was no proof that

Napoleon had repealed his decrees, by March Congress had agreed to Madison's policies and expired. While the nation waited for the Twelfth Congress to assemble, yet another effort at negotiation was made. The British, realizing the extent of American exasperation and themselves in the depths of economic depression, sent a new minister, Augustus Foster, to the United States with instructions to give compensation for the *Chesapeake* affair. This was done by November, but no agreement was reached on the more substantial questions of the Orders in Council and the general practice of impressment.

THE WAR OF 1812

Both President Madison and a substantial number of the Congressmen who gathered in Washington in November 1811 had decided that, unless major concessions were made by Great Britain, the country was obliged to move toward war. This movement progressed slowly and fitfully because it was a war entered into out of desperation. The Republicans had placed all their hopes in the belief that they could sway the policies of the European powers by economic means, and their actions since 1807 had delivered severe blows to the American economy and driven the Federalists into ever more desperate opposition. American military forces were still pitifully weak. The Republicans had moved reluctantly toward moderate increases in the regular army but had still refused to increase the regular navy; it was much weaker than it had been in 1800. There was also still strong Republican opposition to the high taxes that would be necessary if war came. In spite of all this, some Republicans were now convinced that war was necessary to vindicate America's rights to trade freely abroad, to salvage shattered national honor, and to preserve the republic in which such high hopes had been placed.

The new spirit was apparent immediately on the gathering of the new Congress. Henry Clay, who had been the most prominent public spokesman for war, was elected Speaker of the House, although this was his first term in that body. He used his power as Speaker to place supporters of stronger action on the key committees. The group of twenty or so who took the leadership in pressing for war measures became known as the War Hawks. Clay himself was the key figure, and on the Foreign Relations Committee were Peter B. Porter of New York, John C. Calhoun of South Carolina, Felix Grundy of Tennessee, John A. Harper of New Hampshire, and Joseph Desha of Kentucky; these men constituted a majority of the committee. War Hawks also chaired other vital committees: Langdon Cheves of South Carolina headed the Naval committee, David R. Williams of the same state, Military Affairs, and Ezekiel Bacon of Massachusetts, Ways and Means.

In pressing for war measures, Clay also had the support of President Madison. Madison was a more complex thinker than Clay and never had the ability to stir emotions through the written or the spoken word, but he had reluctantly decided that the country was obliged to move toward war. In his annual message to the new Congress he asked its members to put the United States "into an armor and an attitude demanded by the crisis." In response to the President, the Foreign Relations Committee decided to recommend war preparations, not war itself, for the members believed that the United States was simply unprepared to fight. The chairman of the committee, Peter B. Porter, was absolutely clear regarding the material ends that the Republicans sought. "The committee," said Porter, "thought that the Orders in Council, so far as they go to interrupt our direct trade, that is, the carrying of the productions of this country to a market in the ports of friendly nations, and returning with the proceeds of them—ought to be resisted by war." At this moment of crisis, the Foreign Relations Committee tried to emphasize to the farmer supporters of the Republican party that the country was striving for the right to export American farm produce throughout Europe, and in the following debates there was general Republican support for this idea.

At the end of December, Henry Clay stated that "we are assert-ing our claim to the direct trade—the right to export our cotton, tobacco, and other domestic produce to market."

Entwined with the desperation produced by the lack of mar-kets and falling prices was a whole set of fears revolving around the belief that Great Britain intended to keep the young republic in a state of dependence, a dependence enforced by British peacetime and wartime maritime policies, and by influence exerted from Canada. Soon after assembling, Congress heard that full-scale warfare had broken out in the Old Northwest. Governor William Henry Harrison had provoked a battle with the Prophet's forces at Tippecanoe on November 7. The Amer-icans firmly believed that the Indians who fought there were under the influence of British agents from Canada. By invading Canada, the Americans believed they could force a change in British maritime policies while removing a potential threat on America's northern flank. The report of the Foreign Relations Committee made it clear that the United States intended to wage war against Great Britain by an invasion of Canada by land, and by allowing American privateers to harass British commerce at sea.

It has been suggested by some historians, notably that excel-lent diplomatic historian Julius W. Pratt, that some southern Congressmen eventually supported war because of the oppor-tunity it would provide to obtain the Floridas from England's ally Spain. Although the United States desired and eventually expected to get the Floridas, and although the Tennesseans were particularly desirous of attacking West Florida once war was declared, there is little evidence that the desire for Florida played any important part in the decision to declare war. Access to the Gulf had been secured by the Louisiana Purchase, and though Jefferson had failed in his efforts by buy the Floridas, there were increasing signs that their annexation was only a matter of time. For years, Americans had been settling in that part of West Florida directly east of the Mississippi River, and in September 1810, Americans in Baton Rouge staged a coup and offered the region to the United States. In October, Madison promptly annexed West Florida as far as the Perdido River. In 1811 and 1812, American adventurers were penetrating into other parts of the Floridas. There was little that Spain could do about it. The United States declared war to relieve the British stranglehold on the commerce of the new republic, to end perceived British threats to national security, and to refurbish a tarnished national honor, not to attack Spain or its possessions.

The discussions of the war preparations recommended by the Foreign Relations Committee dragged out the move toward war throughout the winter and into the spring of 1812. At heart, the Republicans were anti-war, anti-military, anti-taxation. They were now going to try to achieve by military means what they had failed to achieve through commercial sanctions. Although a core of War Hawks voted for most of the military preparations, most of their Republican colleagues balked at one or other of the war proposals. And while the Republicans bickered, the Federalists relentlessly pointed out the absurdity of war against Great Britain, which they prophesied would complete the ruin of American commerce. They were prepared to vote for some of the measures of military preparedness, but not for war against England.

In the course of the debates, the Republicans made no secret of their basic strategy in the coming war. They were going to force a change in British maritime policies by invading and conquering Canada. It was also clear that if the Americans conquered Canada, there would be considerable sentiment in favor of retaining it. In the debates leading to the war, several of the War Hawks intimated that the old Revolutionary desire to occupy the region still flourished. Richard M. Johnson of Kentucky said of the St. Lawrence that "this great outlet of the northern world, should be at our command, for our convenience and future security," and at the very beginning of the war, Secretary of State James Monroe wrote to the American chargé d'affaires in London that it should be suggested to the British government that it should quickly settle American grievances, for if part of Canada were conquered, public opinion would make it very difficult to give it back. Perhaps the best summary of how Canada was regarded in the coming of the war was given by Charles Ingersoll of Pennsylvania in the House in January 1814. "As a separate cause of war," he said, "independent of all others, I will not undertake to say what the popular sentiment may be with regard to the invasion and conquest of Canada; but, as an instrument for waging it effectually, and as a desirable acquisition in the course of its prosecution, most certainly we do look upon those British provinces in our neighborhood as all-important in the account."

To anticipate conquering Canada was simple, to plan for it was far more difficult. Military preparations progressed slowly in the winter of 1811–1812. On paper Congress had already provided for 10,000 regular troops. After much discussion it was finally agreed in January 1812 that 15,000 more should be raised. Recruiting proceeded slowly, and in June at the beginning of the war there were still less than 10,000 men in the regular army. The navy fared even worse. Even though the Foreign Relations Committee assumed that the war at sea would be waged by privateers, those with a knowledge of naval matters realized that to cope with British blockades and to protect America's coasts, an increased fighting navy was needed. In January 1812, the Naval Committee asked Congress to appropriate money to build twelve ships-of-the-line and twenty frigates. The Republican party was the traditional opponent of a large navy, and some Republicans, even while preparing for war, argued that this force would enhance the power of the American commercial classes without providing the force necessary to meet the British at sea. In spite of Clay's support, the bill for a larger navy was defeated in the lower House, and the United States was to enter the war with a tiny regular navy and no plans for increasing it.

For the Republicans, the answer to all their military problems was to be found in the state militias and in limited term volunteers. Citizen soldiers would wrest Canada from the British and bring the mistress of the ocean to her knees. Yet, even here, traditional Republican principles hampered the war preparations. When the bill to raise 50,000 volunteers was discussed in Congress in January, a major dispute arose as to whether militia could be used outside the United States. By many, the militia was defined as a local defense force. The question of where the militia could be used was of more than minor importance since militia would have to be used to invade Canada, but when the bill passed the question of whether it could be used outside the country was left unanswered. Militia were to be used on attempted invasions of Canada, but some officers and troops were to refuse to cross the border.

The Republican dilemma in shaping measures for war was compounded by the debates on how the war was to be financed. The Ways and Means Committee proposed to finance the war by doubling the customs duties, by imposing internal taxes, by a levy on the states, and by loans. Again the debate was a heated one. Some War Hawks feared that they would get the taxation and no war, and when the bill passed early in March it was with the proviso that the taxes would only be put into effect on the outbreak of war against a European nation. The result of the debates on the regular army and navy, and taxes, combined with the inefficiency of recruitment, was that most of the war preparations would have to take place after the war had begun.

Once the tax bill had passed, Madison was now convinced that war was near, and he took steps to move Congress toward the natural conclusion of its long debates on war measures. In March, he presented to Congress documents which demonstrated that in 1808 and 1809 the Governor in chief of Canada had employed a secret agent in the eastern states. Madison stated that this had been done to foment disaffection, destroy the union, and draw the northeast into a connection with Canada. Madison's opponents said that much of what was disclosed was not new, and that the information was not worth the $50,000 that he had paid for it, but, as Madison had calculated, the effect of his disclosures was to increase the belief that the British crushing of America's foreign commerce was part of an involved system of British hostility aimed at ruining the young republic.

In March 1812, it was generally realized that war with Great Britain was near, although the news that France was still harassing American commerce again produced the remarkable proposal that the United States should declare war on both of the great powers of the world. At least a modicum of good sense prevailed, however, and on April 1, Madison, encouraged to act by Clay and by the Foreign Relations Committee, sent a message to Congress recommending a sixty-day embargo. Such a measure would have the effect of reducing the number of vulnerable American ships at sea if and when the war began. Madison wanted war; he saw no other solution to America's dilemmas. The House passed the bill quickly, but the Senate balked and extended the embargo to ninety days. This was the bill approved by the President on April 4. Madison was now preparing to recommend war, although he was also waiting for dispatches from England to see if the English were prepared to yield on the two essential questions of impressment and the Orders in Council. He heard of no change, and on June 1, sent a recommendation for war to Congress.

Madison's war message listed the grievances against England since 1803. Impressment, illegal blockades, and the seizure of American ships filled most of his message, but he also mentioned the renewal of Indian warfare in the Old Northwest. The declaration of war passed the lower house quickly. Its members had been debating the issue since the previous November. The House was still badly divided. All the Federalists who voted opposed the war, which meant that there was a strong pocket of opposition in the vital states of the northeast. The Republicans who supported the conflict had their most solid strength in the South and West. Kentucky, Tennessee, and Ohio voted for war, and the states from Maryland south to Georgia voted 37 to 11 in favor. The six seaboard states from New Jersey and New York northward opposed the war by a vote of 34 to 14. Vermont was 3 to 1 for war, but the key state was Pennsylvania, which by voting 16 to 2 for war provided the South and West with the margin they needed. The declaration passed by 79 to 49. If the constitution had provided for a two-thirds vote for a declaration of war, it would not have passed. In the Senate, resistance was even stronger, and the declaration finally passed by a vote of only 19 to 13. On June 18, 1812, Madison signed the bill. The United States was at war with Great Britain.

Ironically, just two days before the American declaration of war, the British government had announced that the Orders in Council were to be removed. If this news could have reached America before the war had begun, it would almost certainly have been viewed as a large enough concession to have prevented the declaration of war while further negotiations were held on the subject of impressment. The British had been persuaded to remove the Orders largely as a result of an extremely severe economic depression that had beset the country for the past two years. In an enquiry held by Parliament in the spring, large numbers of merchants and manufacturers had argued that the removal of the Orders in Council and the renewal of American trade would give a sharp stimulus to the economy. The Tory government still resisted change and listened to its shipping and West India interests, but in May the Prime Minister, Spencer Perceval, was assassinated, and the new ministry decided to use the occasion to remove the Orders in Council. The rejoicing of the merchants and manufacturers concerned in the American trade was short-lived, for they were soon to hear the news that the United States had already declared war.

American strategy in the war of 1812 was a failure, although eventually there was limited success in Upper Canada and naval victories on Lake Erie and Lake Champlain. Attempts to conquer Canada in 1812 and 1813 collapsed in a morass of inadequate preparations, difficult terrain, and incompetent leadership. Superficially, the war at sea brought striking successes when the few American frigates won dramatic single-ship engagements, and the fast-sailing, well-manned American privateers caused havoc to British shipping. These successes served to divert attention from the fact that inadequate naval preparations allowed the British to place a stranglehold around the American coastline. By 1813 and 1814, the British blockade ruined American trade and brought the American government to near bankruptcy.

What had begun as a war to bring about a change in British

policies by the invasion and conquest of Canada, by 1814 had become a war for survival. Early in that year Napoleon was defeated, and British ships and troops were sent in large numbers to the New World. The English now were ready to invade the United States and to extort major territorial concessions at a peace treaty. They expected that such concessions would include parts of Maine and control of the southern shores of the Great Lakes. British military plans called for an invasion of Maine; for an invasion force to advance along the Lake Champlain-Hudson River route from Canada to take New York and sever the northeast from the rest of the union; for a force to sail from Jamaica to capture New Orleans; and for a force to engage in diversionary operations in Chesapeake Bay.

A large part of Maine was taken quite easily, and the diversionary force in Chesapeake Bay at first met only token resistance. After landing in Chesapeake Bay in August, the British troops were able to occupy Washington, D.C., and burn the public buildings. They then advanced on Baltimore, but were repulsed. Fortunately for the United States, the major British invasion effort from Canada was a failure. As the army advanced easily to Plattsburg on Lake Champlain, the supporting British naval force was defeated on September 11, 1814, at the battle of Plattsburg Bay. At this, the British army feared for its supply lines and retreated to Canada.

The other main British invasion force that was to sail from Jamaica to capture New Orleans was much delayed, and by the time it was able to proceed, negotiations to end the war were well underway. This was a war in which the diplomatic steps to end it began almost as soon as the war was declared. At the beginning of the war, in June 1812, Secretary of State James Monroe suggested to the American chargé d'affaires in London that an armistice could be arranged if the British would take off the Orders in Council and end impressment. Soon after this, the British instructed their naval commander in chief off the American coast to find out if he could arrange a truce because the British had in fact removed the Orders in Council. These steps did not produce results, for what would have been enough to stop the war from being declared was not enough to stop it once it had actually begun.

A more positive step forward came in September 1812 when the Russians offered mediation through the American minister in St. Petersburg. Napoleon had invaded Russia in June. Russia was now an ally of Great Britain and, being generally in agreement with the United States on commercial matters, wanted to bring the United States and Great Britain together. Communication with Russia was painfully slow, but in March 1813 Madison accepted the Russia offer. By that time, the American government realized that the invasion of Canada was no simple matter, and the British blockade was beginning to hurt. Secretary of the Treasury Albert Gallatin and Senator James A. Bayard of Delaware were appointed to join John Quincy Adams, the American minister in Russia, in peace negotiations. By the time Russia heard of this acceptance in June 1813, Great Britain had declined the offer; she had not the slightest desire to have the question of her maritime rights in time of war mediated by a third power. Thus, the United States now had a peace commission but no one to negotiate with.

In September 1813, Russia renewed her offer to mediate. The British government still was not interested in mediation, but to avoid offending the Russians, the British agreed to negotiate directly with the Americans. On hearing of this, Madison now added Henry Clay and Jonathan Russell, who had been American chargé d'affaires in London, to the peace commission. The Americans were a distinguished group: Swiss-immigrant Gallatin, who had served both Jefferson and Madison as Secretary of the Treasury, was a man of intellectual breadth; Henry Clay had already proved himself to be a man of great political ability as well as great charm; John Quincy Adams had the intelligence and integrity of his father, although he also had the same forbidding New England reserve; Bayard was an extremely talented Federalist. Only Jonathan Russell, the least talented of the Americans, would not have felt out of place as a member of the mediocre British delegation. The major British diplomats were concerned with the settling of peace at the end of the Napoleonic

Wars. The three British delegates—Lord Gambier, Henry Goulburn, and William Adams—referred anything important back to London for decision.

The negotiations were carried out at Ghent in the Netherlands from August to December 1814. Both sides started with lists of demands. The Americans wanted guarantees of neutral rights, the ending of impressment, and large parts of Canada; the British wanted extensive territorial concessions and an Indian buffer state in the Old Northwest. The Americans were so pessimistic at the chance of an agreement that late in August they prepared to leave Ghent, but the British encouraged the Americans to continue discussions. The British government hoped that news of decisive British victories in America would force the Americans to yield to British demands. In October, when news arrived that Washington had been burned, it appeared that British hopes had been realized, but quickly news followed that the British army had retreated from Baltimore, and, more significantly, that the British invasion of the United States from Canada had failed at Plattsburg.

The British were now anxious to extricate themselves from a war that was costing a great deal of money and which seemed to be settling into a military stalemate. In November, in the hope of achieving some solution, the British cabinet asked the most famous British soldier, the Duke of Wellington, for his views of the military situation and offered to give him the command in Canada. His answer hastened the coming of peace, for he said that he could do little in Canada without naval control of the Great Lakes and that, given the existing military position, Great Britain was not justified in asking for territorial cessions. In November and December, both the British and the Americans abandoned any hope of obtaining concessions from the other power, and on December 24, the treaty of Ghent was signed. The treaty provided for the mutual restoration of any conquered territory and for four mixed commissions to deal with the problems regarding different parts of the United States-Canadian boundary. Nothing was said in the treaty about neutral rights or impressment, or about American commerce in general, although in 1815 Clay and Gallatin signed a commercial agreement in London, which in essence renewed the provisions of Jay's Treaty that had fallen into abeyance in 1807.

The war had begun with the United States wanting to change British maritime policies by the conquest of Canada; it ended with the Americans desperately resisting British invasion forces. Yet, in spite of this, the United States viewed the War of 1812 as a success and celebrated it as "the second war of independence." The United States was able to do this because of the peculiar circumstances of the last year of the war. By August 1814, the condition of the United States was at its nadir. The attempts to invade Canada had failed disastrously, American commerce had been ruined by the British blockade, the treasury was empty, Washington was in flames, and large British invasion forces were advancing from Canada and assembling in Jamaica. And then, magically, all was transformed. The British were repulsed from Baltimore, retreated from Plattsburg, and ultimately, in January 1815, failed disastrously before New Orleans.

This last event was the most miraculous of all. The British began to land near New Orleans at the beginning of December. While the negotiators at Ghent were winding up their business, the British troops came ashore and skirmished with the Americans. Finally, two weeks after the peace was signed, but before they had heard of it, the British launched a frontal attack on Andrew Jackson's positions near New Orleans. They were thrown back in utter confusion; the British suffered some two thousand casualties, the Americans less than one hundred. News of this great victory and of the peace of Ghent reached the East at about the same time. The two events were irrevocably linked in American minds. The United States had ended its "second war of independence" in triumph. The disasters of the first two years of the war were forgotten. What had begun as a war to vindicate American maritime rights and nationhood by the conquest of Canada was finally viewed as successful because the British invasion of America had failed.

In the years after 1776 the United States had sought independence, security, and commercial and territorial expansion. By 1815, the country had taken large strides toward achieving all of its objectives. The most striking successes had been achieved on the North American Continent. Access to the Gulf, a settled boundary on the Great Lakes, and the Louisiana Purchase had ensured continued and dramatic westward expansion. In this respect American diplomats had dealt effectively with European nations deeply embroiled in the widespread wars sweeping their own continent. The effect of the European wars on American trade had been more complex. Extraordinary wartime conditions had provided dramatic opportunities for an expansion of American exports and the American carrying trade, but had also produced the large-scale interference with neutral trade that had provoked bitter reactions in the United States. From 1807 to 1815 American trade had been badly hurt by the Republican efforts to change the maritime policies of the European belligerents. In these years, immediate economic self-interest was in large part sacrificed to national pride and to an unrealistic hope of forcing foreign powers, particularly England, to allow American trade widespread latitude in war as well as in peace. Yet, the economic dislocations of the 1807–1815 period were only temporary and in the following years were to be succeeded by a period of dramatic growth.

For much of the time from 1783 to 1815 the United States had feared for its security. There had been an apprehension that the country would not be able to forge an instrument of centralized government that could maintain internal unity while securing the nation from foreign enemies anxious to take advantage of America's weakness. By 1815 these doubts had been resolved, and in the following years the United States was able to realize the dreams that had inspired Americans at the very beginning of the Revolution; dreams of a vast nation spanning the continent and trading with the world. After 1815 it was no longer American security that was in question but the security of the areas adjacent to the United States on the North American Continent, and while pioneers thrust outward across America, American shipping penetrated the oceans of the world.

Bibliographical Essay

The colonial background of early American diplomacy has been discussed in most detail in the writings of Max Savelle. His fullest account is in *The Origins of American Diplomacy: The International History of Angloamerica, 1492-1763* (New York, 1967), but more interpretive are his "Colonial Origins of American Diplomatic Principles," *Pacific Historical Review,* 3 (Sept. 1934): 334-350, and "The American Balance of Power and European Diplomacy, 1713-1778," in Richard B. Morris, ed., *The Era of the American Revolution* (New York, 1939), 140-169. The most influential work on the intellectual origins of early American foreign policy has been Felix Gilbert, *To the*

Farewell Address: Ideas of Early American Foreign Policy (Princeton, N.J., 1961). Gilbert is particularly interested in the European origins of American foreign policy. He argues that American foreign policy was idealistic and internationalist as well as isolationist, and that in the early years of the new republic there was a tension between Idealism and Realism. Less concerned with the shaping of American foreign policy, but basic to the placing of the new American nation within its general trans-Atlantic context is Robert R. Palmer, *The Age of the Democratic Revolution: A Political History of Europe and America, 1760-1800,* 2 vols. (Princeton, N.J., 1959-1964).

A number of works provide general accounts or interpretations of American foreign policy in the first decades of the new nation. Two well-written books which between them cover this entire era are Lawrence S. Kaplan, *Colonies into Nation: American Diplomacy, 1763-1801* (New York, 1972), and Paul A. Varg, *Foreign Policies of the Founding Fathers* (East Lansing, Mich., 1963). Varg is interested in the ways in which American ideals were tempered by the problems of shaping actual policy. Arthur B. Darling, *Our Rising Empire, 1763-1803* (New Haven, 1940; reprinted, 1962) is still of use. Of value for placing American diplomacy within its general political context are John C. Miller, *The Federalist Era, 1789-1801* (New York, 1960), and Marshall Smelser, *The Democratic Republic, 1801-1815* (New York, 1968).

While many of the diplomatic historians of early national America have been concerned with such general themes as the conflict between idealism and realism, isolationism, or the degree to which the young United States acted in an innovative or traditional manner in its foreign policy, others have argued vigorously that the new republic was a driving expansionist power. In his book *The Rising American Empire* (New York, 1960), Richard W. Van Alstyne is particularly concerned with the territorial ambitions of Americans and their government, while in *The Roots of the Modern American Empire: A Study of the Growth and Shaping of Social Consciousness in a Marketplace Society* (New York, 1969) William Appleman Williams depicts a nation driven by agrarian-commercial motives. Williams argues that the agrarian majority in the United States wanted more land for agricultural production as well as the vigorous expansion of its international markets. More tightly argued is his article "The Age of Mercantilism: An Interpretation of the American Political Economy, 1763–1828," *William and Mary Quarterly,* 3rd ser., 15 (Oct. 1958): 419–437, in which he contends that the United States was mercantilist in the ways in which it sought a favorable balance of trade and that James Madison was the leading figure in this movement.

The standard account of the diplomacy of the Revolution has long been Samuel F. Bemis, *The Diplomacy of the American Revolution* (1935; rev. ed., Bloomington, Inc., 1957). This work is nationalistic in tone, but Bemis's work is rich in archival research. For the negotiations leading to the peace of Paris the fullest account is Richard B. Morris, *The Peacemakers: The Great Powers and American Independence* (New York, 1965). Franklin's motives in Paris, as well as his entire thought on foreign policy, are treated effectively in Gerald Stourzh, *Benjamin Franklin and American Foreign Policy* (2d, ed., Chicago, 1969). Readable, but less useful for understanding Franklin's thought is Cecil B. Currey, *Code Number 72/Ben Franklin: Patriot or Spy?* (Englewood Cliffs, N.J., 1972) in which Carey argues that Franklin was working for the British while American minister to France. John Jay has attracted considerably less attention than Franklin, but there is much on Jay as a diplomat in Frank Monaghan, *John Jay: Defender of Liberty* (New York, 1935). Robert R. Livingston, the American Secretary of Foreign Affairs in the last years of the Revolution, is the subject of an excellently written biography by George Dangerfield: *Chancellor Robert R. Livingston of New York, 1746–1813* (New York, 1960). This biography is also useful for the negotiations leading to the Louisiana Purchase.

John Adams has attracted nearly as much interest as Franklin. In *John Adams and the Diplomacy of the American Revolution* (Lexington, Ky., 1980). James H. Hutson argues that Adams's ideas were shaped by traditional balance-of-power considerations, and that his diplomatic maneuvers were also affected by his paranoia. In his other writings on the diplomacy of the Revolution, Hutson has disagreed with Felix Gilbert's contention that the young republic was inspired, at least in part, by idealistic internationalism. In his "Intellectual Foundations of Early American Diplomacy," *Diplomatic History,* I (Winter 1977): 1–19, he contends that the United States shaped her policies within the framework of contemporary European power politics. Also of value for understanding American revolutionary diplomacy are Hutson's "The Partition Treaty and the Declaration of American Independence," *Journal of American History,* 58 (March 1972): 877–896, and "Early American Diplomacy: A Reappraisal," in Lawrence S. Kaplan, ed., *The American Revolution and "A Candid World"* (Kent, Ohio, 1977), 40–68. This Kaplan volume contains several other essays discussing American diplomacy during the Revolution, including William C. Stinchcombe, "John Adams and the Model Treaty, *ibid.,* 111–133; and Lawrence S. Kaplan, "Toward Isolationism: The Rise and Fall of the Franco-American Alliance, 1775–1801," *ibid.,* 134–160.

The attempt to win French support and the eventual Franco-American alliance are discussed in *The American Revolution and the French Alliance* (Syracuse, N.Y., 1969), by William C. Stinchcombe, who is particularly concerned with American perceptions of the connection. Jonathan R. Dull in *The French Navy and American Independence: A Study of Arms and Diplomacy, 1774–1787* (Princeton, N.J., 1975) concentrates on the shaping of French policy. There are several useful essays in Ronald Hoffman and Peter J. Albert, eds., *Diplomacy and Revolution: The Franco-American Alliance of 1778* (Charlottesville, 1981). Richard W. Van Alstyne goes beyond France to discuss the whole international context in *Empire and Independence: The International History of the American Revolution* (New York, 1965). Although most of Van Alstyne's writings are vigorously argued, this book has more detail than interpretation. American-Dutch relations are treated effectively in Jan Willem Schulte Nordholt, *The Dutch Republic and American Independence,* trs. by Herbert H. Rowen (Chapel Hill, N.C., 1982).

The diplomatic history of the Confederation has been treated less effectively than that of the Revolution or the years after 1789. A good beginning, however, is provided by Frederick W. Marks, *Independence on Trial: Foreign Affairs and the Making of the Constitution* (Baton Rouge, 1973). Marks is particularly interested in the degree to which problems in foreign affairs helped swell the demand for a stronger central government.

Postwar difficulties with England can be followed in Charles R. Ritcheson, *Aftermath of Revolution: British Policy Toward the United States, 1783-1795* (Dallas, 1969). Ritcheson argues that the United States and Great Britain had an underlying community of interest. The idea of underlying economic, social, and cultural factors drawing the United States and England together has influenced a number of historians writing on Anglo-American relations in these years. The ways in which common trans-Atlantic interests were developed in the years from 1790 to 1850 is discussed in the essays in Frank Thistlethwaite, *The Anglo-American Connection in the Early Nineteenth Century* (Philadelphia, 1959). Vincent T. Harlow, *The Founding of the Second British Empire, 1763-1973.* Vol. 1. *Discovery and Revolution* (London, 1952) is particularly useful on the shaping of postwar British attitudes toward the United States.

Basic for an understanding of the problems with Spain in the years after the Revolution are two older works: Arthur P. Whitaker, *The Spanish-American Frontier, 1783-1795: The Westward Movement and the Spanish Retreat in the Mississippi Valley* (Boston, 1927), and Samuel F. Bemis, *Pinckney's Treaty: America's Advantage from Europe's Distress, 1783-1800* (1926; rev. ed., New Haven, 1960). In "Pinckney's Treaty: A New Perspective," *Hispanic American Historical Review,* 43 (Nov. 1963): 526-535, Raymond A. Young reexamines the reasons for Spain's willingness to sign a treaty.

Discussions of foreign policy in the Federalist era are abundant. Many works have dealt with the detailed diplomatic relations with the different European countries, particularly France and England, but there has also been a good deal of interest in the different concepts of foreign policy represented by the aims and attitudes of Alexander Hamilton and Thomas Jefferson. There is much of value on the shaping of American foreign policy in the 1790s in Gerald Stourzh, *Alexander Hamilton and the Idea of Republican Government* (Stanford, Calif., 1970), and in J. G. A. Pocock, *The Machiavellian Moment: Florentine Political Thought and the Atlantic Republican Tradition* (Princeton, N.J., 1975). Gilbert L. Lycan, *Alexander Hamilton and American Foreign Policy: A Design for Greatness* (Norman, Okla., 1970) is very favorable to Hamilton. In *Number 7: Alexander Hamilton's Secret Attempts to Control American Foreign Policy* (Princeton, N.J., 1964), Julian P. Boyd argues that Hamilton undermined Jefferson's policies as Secretary of State by secret contacts with British envoys in the United States.

The shaping of an opposition to Hamilton's pro-British orientation of American foreign policy is considered in two articles: Merrill D. Peterson, "Thomas Jefferson and Commercial Policy, 1783–1793," *William and Mary Quarterly,* 3rd ser., 22 (Oct. 1965): 584–610, and Drew McCoy, "Republicanism and American Foreign Policy: James Madison and the Political Economy of Commercial Discrimination, 1789 to 1794," *William and Mary Quarterly,* 3rd ser., 31 (Oct. 1974): 633–646. In "The Consensus of 1789: Jefferson and Hamilton on American Foreign Policy," *South Atlantic Quarterly,* 71 (Winter 1972): 91–105, Lawrence S. Kaplan discusses the degree to which Hamilton and Jefferson agreed on long-term American objectives.

The problems produced for American shipping and seamen by the outbreak of general European war in 1793 has generated extensive writing, and several older works are useful for discussions of maritime problems. Among these are Walter Alison Phillips and Arthur H. Reede, *Neutrality: Its History, Economics, and Law,* vol. II, *The Napoleonic Period* (New York, 1936); Anna C. Clauder, *American Commerce as Affected by the Wars of the French Revolution and Napoleon, 1793–1812* (Philadelphia, 1932); and James F. Zimmerman, *Impressment of American Seamen* (New York, 1925). Zimmerman's work is still the only book-length study of impressment. The British

point of view on this controversial subject is given in two articles
by Anthony Steel: "Anthony Merry and the Anglo-American
Dispute about Impressment, 1803-6," *Cambridge Historical
Journal,* 9: 3 (1949): 331-351, and "Impressment in the Monroe-Pinkney Negotiations, 1806-1807," *American Historical
Review,* 57 (Jan. 1952): 352-369. The problems and successes of
one phase of American-European trade in these troubled years
are presented in Alfred W. Crosby, Jr., *America, Russia,
Hemp, and Napoleon: American Trade with Russia and the Baltic, 1783-1812* (Columbus, Ohio, 1965).

The crisis with England, Jay's Treaty, and the subsequent
rapprochement between the United States and Great Britain are
effectively treated in three volumes. The classic description of
the problems and negotiations leading to Jay's Treaty is that of
Samuel F. Bemis, *Jay's Treaty: A Study in Commerce and
Diplomacy* (1923; 2d ed., New Haven, 1962). The political
impact of the treaty is probed in Jerald A. Combs, *The Jay
Treaty: Political Battleground of the Founding Fathers* (Berke-
ley, Calif., 1970). For the marked improvement in relations with
England after Jay's Treaty, the standard work is Bradford
Perkins, *The First Rapprochement: England and the United
States, 1795-1805* (Philadelphia, 1955).

Relations with France, and the declining effectiveness of the
French alliance, have formed the main theme of a number of
works. There is little analysis in Louis M. Sears, *George
Washington and the French Revolution* (Detroit, 1960), which is
organized in a strictly chronological manner. A useful introduc-
tion to the variety of interpretations of Washington's Farewell
Address is Arthur A. Markowitz, "Washington's Farewell and
the Historians: A Critical Review," *Pennsylvania Magazine of
History and Biography,* 94 (April 1970): 173-191. In *The
Struggle for Neutrality: Franco-American Diplomacy During
the Federalist Era* (Knoxville, Tenn., 1974), Albert Hall
Bowman demonstrates how the Federalists helped bring about
the end of the French alliance. This is also a major theme in
Alexander DeConde, *Entangling Alliance: Politics and
Diplomacy under George Washington* (Durham, N.C., 1958).
DeConde argues that President Washington was dominated by

Hamilton and his ideas. DeConde is also critical of Federalist policies in *The Quasi-War: The Politics and Diplomacy of the Undeclared Naval War with France, 1797–1801* (New York, 1966). These same years are also discussed in detail, and the often-attacked Timothy Pickering somewhat rehabilitated in Gerald A. Clarfield, *Timothy Pickering and American Diplomacy, 1795–1800* (Columbia, Mo., 1969).

Three articles which are useful in depicting special aspects of the diplomacy of the Adams presidency are Thomas C. Ray, "'Not One Cent for Tribute': The Public Addresses and American Popular Reaction to the XYZ Affair, 1798–1799," *Journal of the Early Republic,* 3 (Winter 1983): 389–412. Frederick B. Tolles, "Unofficial Ambassador: George Logan's Mission to France, 1798," *William and Mary Quarterly,* 3rd ser., 7 (Jan. 1950): 3–25; and Stephen G. Kurtz, "The French Mission of 1799–1800: Concluding Chapter in the Statecraft of John Adams," *Political Science Quarterly,* 80 (Dec. 1965): 543–557. In his book *The XYZ Affair* (Westport, Conn., 1980), William C. Stinchcombe analyzes both American and French policies.

Many of the diplomats employed in the various special missions of the 1790's have received individual treatment. Among the relevant studies are Harry Ammon, *James Monroe: The Quest for National Identity* (New York, 1971); George A. Billias, *Elbridge Gerry: Founding Father and Republican Statesman* (New York, 1976); Peter P. Hill, *William Vans Murray, Federalist Diplomat: The Shaping of Peace with France, 1797–1801* (Syracuse, N.Y., 1971); and Marvin R. Zahniser, *Charles Cotesworth Pinckney, Founding Father* (Chapel Hill, N.C., 1967). Secretary of States Edmund Randolph is treated favorably in John J. Reardon, *Edmund Randolph: A Biography* (New York, 1974).

The diplomatic history of the presidencies of Thomas Jefferson and James Madison has often been cast in terms of the causes of the War of 1812, but there has also been considerable interest in the Louisiana question and in the problems with Spain in the Floridas. There is much of use for the diplomatic history of these years in Merrill D. Peterson's standard one volume biography of Jefferson: *Thomas Jefferson and the New Nation: a Biography* (New York, 1970). Special aspects of Jefferson and foreign policy are dealt with in books by Lawrence S. Kaplan and Reginald C. Stuart. In his *Jefferson and France: An Essay on Politics and Political Ideas* (New Haven, 1967), Kaplan depicts Jefferson's as committed to a pro-French policy to such an extent as to cloud his judgment. In *The Half-Way Pacifist: Thomas Jefferson's View of War* (Toronto, 1978), Reginald Stuart points out that Jefferson was prepared to go to war if he believed it necessary. Stuart has also expanded his discussion beyond Jefferson in his *War and American Thought: From the Revolution to the Monroe Doctrine* (Kent, Ohio, 1982). Problems of war and diplomacy are also considered, from a more legalistic point of view, in Abraham D. Sofaer, *War, Foreign Affairs, and Constitutional Power: The Origins* (Cambridge, Mass., 1976). In this volume Sofaer is particularly concerned with the role of the President, and concentrates on the early national period. Richard E. Ellis in "The Political Economy of Thomas Jefferson," Lally Weymouth, ed., *Thomas Jefferson: The Man, His World, His Influence* (New York, 1973), 81-95, discusses Jefferson's interest in agricultural expansion and markets, and argues that Jefferson not Hamilton was the realist. The fullest account of James Madison as Secretary of State is in Irving Brant's multi-volume biography of Jefferson's friend and colleague. Relevant for the Jefferson years is *James Madison: Secretary of State, 1800–1809* (Indianapolis, 1953). Brant is extremely favorable to Madison.

The two main foreign policy problems of Jefferson's first term—the war with Tripoli and the Louisiana Purchase—have both attracted the attention of historians. The Barbary powers were a constant problem for the United States in the years from 1783 to 1815. The whole question is considered in Ray W. Irwin, *The Diplomatic Relations of the United States with the Barbary Powers, 1776-1816* (Chapel Hill, N.C., 1931). The difficulties of the Confederation and Washington's presidency are dealt with effectively in H. G. Barnaby, *The Prisoners of Algiers: An Account of the Forgotten American-Algerian War, 1785-1797* (New York, 1966). There is more on diplomatic matters in this book than is implied by its title. Most useful for the problems with Tripoli under Jefferson is Louis B. Wright and Julia H. Macleod, *The First Americans in North Africa: William Eaton's Struggle for a Vigorous Policy Against the Barbary Pirates, 1799–1805* (Princeton, N.J., 1945).

The standard book on the Louisiana Purchase is Alexander DeConde, *This Affair of Louisiana* (New York, 1976). DeConde relates the purchase to the history of American expansionism in the early national period. Several older volumes are also still of use: E. Wilson Lyon, *Louisiana in French Diplomacy, 1759–1804* (Norman, Okla., 1934); the same author's, *The Man Who Sold Louisiana: The Career of François Barbé-Marbois* (Norman, Okla., 1942); and Arthur P. Whitaker, *The Mississippi Question, 1795–1803: A Study in Trade, Politics, and Diplomacy* (New York, 1934). There is also information on the Louisiana Purchase, and on the subsequent problems regarding the Floridas in Joseph T. Hatfield, *William Claiborne: Jeffersonian Centurion in the Southwest* (Lafayette, La., 1976), and in Jared W. Bradley, "W.C.C. Claiborne and Spain: Foreign Affairs under Jefferson and Madison, 1801–1811," *Louisiana History,* 12 (Fall 1971): 287–314; 13 (Winter 1972): 5–26.

Still useful on the details of the West Florida controversy is Isaac J. Cox, *The West Florida Controversy, 1798–1813: A Study in American Diplomacy* (Baltimore, 1918). A more modern interpretation, based on work in the French archives, is presented in Clifford L. Egan, "The United States, France, and West Florida, 1803–1807," *Florida Historical Quarterly,* 47 (Jan. 1969): 227–253, and in Wanjohi Waciuma, *Intervention in Spanish Floridas, 1801–1813: A Study in Jeffersonian Foreign Policy* (Boston, 1976). All of these writers are critical of the conduct of the American government. Rembert W. Patrick, *Florida Fiasco: Rampant Rebels on the Georgia-Florida border, 1810–1815* (Athens, Geo., 1954) is a lively account, which is also critical of American policy.

Much of the writing discussing American diplomatic history in the years from 1803 to 1812 is concerned in one way or another with the causes of the War of 1812. The historiographical arguments, which have swayed back and forth for the past sixty years, are discussed in three articles: Warren H. Goodman, "The Origins of the War of 1812: A Survey of Changing Interpretations," *Mississippi Valley Historical Review,* 28 (Sept. 1941): 171–186; Reginald Horsman, "Western War Aims, 1811–1812," *Indiana Magazine of History,* 53 (March 1957): 1–18; and Clifford L. Egan, "The Origins of the War of 1812: Three Decades of Historical Writing," *Military Affairs,* 38 (April 1974): 72–75.

The fullest accounts of United States diplomatic relations with England and France respectively in these years are Bradford Perkins, *Prologue to War: England and the United States, 1805–1812* (Berkeley, Calif., 1961), and Clifford L. Egan, *Neither Peace Nor War: Franco-American Relations, 1803–1812* (Baton Rouge, La., 1983). Useful for the details of diplomatic representation in France and England are Robert Ernst, *Rufus King: American Federalist* (Chapel Hill, N.C., 1968); C. Edward Skeen, *John Armstrong, Jr., 1758–1843: A Biography* (Syracuse, N.Y., 1981); and Irving Brant, "Joel Barlow, Madison's Stubborn Minister," *William and Mary Quarterly,* 3rd ser., 15 (Oct. 1958): 438–451.

The nature of the commercial warfare is effectively depicted in two older studies: Eli F. Hecksher, *The Continental System: An Economic Interpretation* (Oxford, 1922), and Frank E. Melvin, *Napoleon's Navigation System: A Study of Trade Control During the Continental Blockade* (New York, 1919). Geoffrey Ellis, *Napoleon's Continental Blockade: The Case of Alsace* (Oxford, 1981) has a useful survey of earlier writing about the blockade. A good analysis of the degree to which the American government had difficulty in enforcing economic coercion is given in Herbert Heaton, "Non-Importation, 1806–1812," *Journal of Economic History,* I (Nov. 1941): 178–198. Jefferson's Embargo has long fascinated historians. In the latest study—*Jefferson's English Crisis: Commerce, Embargo, and the Republican Revolution* (Charlottesville, Va., 1979)—Burton Spivak argues that Jefferson originally wanted war in 1807, and conceived of the Embargo as a means of preparing for such a conflict by keeping American merchant ships in port. Only later, he argues, did Jefferson think of the Embargo as a coercive measure. Two older studies are still of use. Walter W. Jennings, *The American Embargo, 1807-1809* (Iowa City, 1921) is particularly concerned with the economic effects of the Embargo in the United States. In *Jefferson and the Embargo* (Durham, N.C., 1927), Louis M. Sears argues that Jefferson used the Embargo in an attempt to coerce Europe peacefully. Robin D. S. Higham, "The Port of Boston and the Embargo of 1807-1809," *American Neptune,* 16 (July 1956): 189-210, presents evidence that supports Heaton's argument that trade continued in spite of commercial restrictions. The economic effectiveness of the Embargo is defended in Jeffrey A. Frankel, "The 1807-1809 Embargo Against Great Britain," *Journal of Economic History,* 42 (June 1982): 291-308. See also Richard Mannix, "Gallatin, Jefferson, and the Embargo of 1808," *Diplomatic History,* 3 (Spring 1979): 151-172.

From the mid-1920s until the 1960s the most accepted interpretation of the causes of the War of 1812 was that presented by Julius W. Pratt in *The Expansionists of 1812* (New York, 1925; reprinted, 1949). Pratt argues that one essential ingredient in the coming of the War of 1812 was an alliance between Westerners and Southerners for expansionist purposes. Westerners desired to invade Canada to remove British backing of the Indians, and Southerners desired the Floridas for agrarian, commercial, and strategic reasons. In two articles in the early 1930s George R. Taylor argued that the West had a vital interest in British commercial regulations, which they blamed for their agrarian distress. His "Prices in the Mississippi Valley Preceding the War of 1812," *Journal of Economic and Business History,* 3 (1930): 148-163, contains data demonstrating the depressed state of prices at New Orleans from 1808 to 1812, and in his "Agrarian Discontent in the Mississippi Valley Preceding the War of 1812," *Journal of Political Economy,* 39 (Aug. 1931): 471-505, he shows that the Westerners blamed European commercial restrictions for their problems. This maritime interpretation of the coming of the war was given additional support by Alfred L. Burt in *The United States, Great Britain and British North America from the Revolution to the Establishment of Peace after the War of 1812* (New Haven, 1940). In her article "South

Carolina—A Protagonist of the War of 1812," *American Historical Review,* 61 (July 1956): 914-929, Margaret K. Latimer demonstrates that Taylor's arguments regarding agrarian discontent also applied to South Carolina.

Through the 1950s Pratt's expansionist arguments still exerted considerable influence, but in the early 1960s some of the arguments suggested by Taylor, Burt, and Latimer were extended and reshaped, and new interpretations advanced, to present a general attack on the expansionist thesis. Among these studies were Bradford Perkins, *Prologue to War: England and the United States, 1805-1812* (Berkeley, Calif., 1961); Reginald Horsman, *The Causes of the War of 1812* (Philadelphia, 1962); reprinted, 1972); and Roger H. Brown, *The Republic in Peril: 1812* (New York, 1964). Perkins uses extensive research in British as well as American archives to criticize Republican leadership, but generally suggests a maritime interpretation of the war. Horsman also argues that the war stemmed from maritime causes, and maintains that Canada was invaded primarily in the hope of forcing a change in British maritime policies, not to stop British support of the Indians. Brown, in his detailed study of the Twelfth Congress, argues that party, not sectional, factors were of vital importance in the coming of the war (in this agreeing with Perkins), and also argues that a basic reason for the war was the Republican fear that republicanism itself was in peril.

In addition to the book-length defenses of the maritime interpretation, a number of articles in the 1960s refined the interpretations of the coming of the war. In his "1812: Conservatives, War Hawks, and the Nation's Honor," *William and Mary Quarterly,* 3rd ser., 18 (April 1961): 196-210, Norman K. Risjord contends that a desire to defend national honor not commercial difficulties or expansionism was at the heart of the decision for war in 1812. In his "France and Madison's Decision for War, 1812," *Mississippi Valley Historical Review,* 50 (March 1964): 652-671, Lawrence S. Kaplan demonstrates that the Republicans had no desire for an alliance with France. The House vote for war in 1812 has attracted the most attention, but the difficulties of achieving a vote for war in the Senate are discussed in Leland R. Johnson, "The Suspense Was Hell: The Senate Vote for the War of 1812," *Indiana Magazine of History,* 65 (Dec. 1969): 247–267.

The role of the War Hawks in the coming of the war has attracted special attention in several of the articles published in the 1960s and 1970s. In "The War Hawks and the War of 1812," *Indiana Magazine of History,* 60 (June 1964): 119–158, which is a publication of the revised proceedings of a session of the Mississippi Valley Historical Association, conflicting points of view are included. Reginald Horsman identifies the War Hawks by tabulating and analyzing votes in the first session of the 12th Congress, Roger Brown denies that there were any real War Hawks, and Alexander DeConde and Norman Risjord comment. Discussion of the War Hawks has continued in two more recent articles. Ronald L. Hatzenbuehler, "The War Hawks and the Question of Congressional Leadership in 1812," *Pacific Historical Review,* 45 (Feb. 1976): 1–22, uses quantitative techniques to identify the War Hawks, and discusses their relationship with the executive. In "The War Hawks of 1812: Party Leadership in the Twelfth Congress," *Capitol Studies,* 5 (Spring 1977): 25–42, Harry W. Fritz argues that the War Hawks played a vital role in the coming of the war. For an understanding of the leading War Hawk, Henry Clay, there is much of value in Bernard Mayo's lively, well-written account of young Henry Clay, *Henry Clay: Spokesman of the New West* (Boston, 1937).

In *Congress Declares War: Rhethoric, Leadership, and Partisanship in the Early Republic* (Kent, Ohio, 1983), Ronald L. Hatzenbuehler and Robert L. Ivie examine the dynamics that led Congress to the declaration of war. Hatzenbuehler's "Party Unity and the Decision for War in the House of Representatives, 1812," *William and Mary Quarterly,* 3rd ser., 29 (July 1972): 376–390, gives support to the views of Perkins and Brown that the vote for war can best be explained in party rather than sectional terms.

Along with the War Hawks, there has been an interest in the role of Madison in the coming of the war, and in his relationship with Congress and its committees. Madison's detailed actions, viewed in a favorable light, can be followed in Irving Brant, *James Madison: The President, 1809-1812* (Indianapolis, 1956). In "Mr. Madison's War and Long-Term Congressional Voting Behavior," *William and Mary Quarterly,* 3rd ser., 36 (July 1979): 373-395, Rudolph M. Bell analyzes voting patterns and argues that Madison was vital to the actual declaration of war. The importance of Madison in the coming of the war is also defended in J.C.A. Stagg, "James Madison and the 'Malcontents': The Political Origins of the War of 1812," *William and Mary Quarterly,* 3rd ser., 33 (Oct. 1976): 557-585. In a second article: "James Madison and the Coercion of Great Britain: Canada, the West Indies, and the War of 1812," *William and Mary Quarterly,* 3rd ser., 38 (Jan. 1981): 3-34, Stagg argues that Madison wanted to invade Canada because of its commercial importance for the British and thus for American commercial warfare. In his book *Mr. Madison's War: Politics, Diplomacy, and Warfare in the Early American Republic, 1783-1830* (Princeton, N.J., 1983), Stagg amplifies the arguments contained in the articles as well as examining in detail the problems of mobilizing American society for the war.

Among the abundant writings on the coming of the War of 1812, there are a number of discussions of individual states. Two useful full-length studies are Victor A. Sapio, *Pennsylvania and the War of 1812* (Lexington, 1970), and Sarah McCulloh Lemmon, *Frustrated Patriots: North Carolina and the War of 1812* (Chapel Hill, N.C., 1973). Sapio concentrates on the coming of the war, while Lemmon devotes much of her attention to the participation of the state in the war itself. Among the articles that deal with specific states or regions are Robert V. Haynes, "The Southwest and the War of 1812," *Louisiana History,* 5 (Winter 1964): 41-51; William R. Barlow, "Ohio's Congressmen and the War of 1812," *Ohio History,* 72 (July 1963): 175-194; and the same author's "The Coming of the War of 1812 in Michigan Territory," *Michigan History,* 53 (Summer, 1969): 91-107.

Diplomacy during the War of 1812, and the negotiations

resulting in the treaty of Ghent have attracted less attention than the coming of the war. In *The War of 1812* (New York, 1969), Reginald Horsman discusses military factors bearing on the eventual peace treaty. The most effective analysis of the negotiations leading to the treaty of Ghent is in Bradford Perkins, *Castlereagh and Adams: England and the United States, 1812–1823* (Berkeley, Calif., 1964). Fred L. Engelman's *The Peace of Christmas Eve* (New York, 1962) is a detailed, readable account, and Frank A. Updyke, *The Diplomacy of the War of 1812* (Baltimore, 1915) is less readable, but contains details that cannot easily be found elsewhere. George Dangerfield, *The Era of Good Feelings* (New York, 1952) has an insightful discussion of the Ghent negotiations. Two older articles that discuss special aspects of the negotiations are still of use: F. A. Golder, "The Russian Offer of Mediation in the War of 1812," *Political Science Quarterly,* 31 (Sept. 1916): 380–391, is still of value because it is based on work in the Russian archives, and Charles M. Gates, "The West in American Diplomacy, 1812–1815," *Mississippi Valley Historical Review,* 26 (March 1940): 499–510, discusses the British barrier state project as well as American objectives.

For additional references to writings on American diplomatic history in these years, the standard compilation is Richard Dean Burns, ed., *Guide to American Foreign Relations Since 1700* (Santa Barbara, 1983). This can be supplemented by Gerald K. Haines and J. Samuel Walker, eds., *American Foreign Relations: A Historiographical Review* (Westport, Conn., 1981), and Norman A. Graebner, ed., *American Diplomatic History before 1900* (Arlington Heights, Ill., 1978). The ways in which American diplomatic historians have approached their subject is discussed in Jerald A. Combs, *American Diplomatic History: Two Centuries of Changing Interpretations* (Berkeley, Calif., 1982).

INDEX